Slavery
Throughout History
Primary Sources

Slavery
Throughout History
Primary Sources

Judson Knight

AN IMPRINT OF THE GALE GROUP

DETROIT · NEW YORK · SAN FRANCISCO
LONDON · BOSTON · WOODBRIDGE, CT

Judson Knight

Staff

Julie L. Carnagie, *U•X•L Senior Editor*
Carol DeKane Nagel, *U•X•L Managing Editor*
Thomas Romig, *U•X•L Publisher*
Erin Bealmear, *Permissions Associate*

Randy Bassett, *Image Database Supervisor*
Robert Duncan, *Imaging Specialist*
Pamela A. Reed, *Image Coordinator*
Kelly A. Quin, *Image Editor*

Pamela A. E. Galbreath, *Senior Art Director*
Tracey Rowens, *Art Director*

Evi Seoud, *Assistant Manager, Composition Purchasing and Electronic Prepress*
Mary Beth Trimper, *Manager, Composition and Electronic Prepress*

Rita Wimberley, *Senior Buyer*
Dorothy Maki, *Manufacturing Manager*

Marco Di Vita, Graphix Group, *Typesetting*

Cover photographs (from top to bottom): Child laborer reproduced by permission of AP/Wide World Photos, Inc.; Sudanese slaves reproduced by permission of Reuters/Stringer/ Archive Photos.

Library of Congress Cataloging-in-Publication Data

Slavery throughout history: primary sources / [compiled by] Judson Knight.
   p. cm.
   Includes bibliographical references and index.
   ISBN 0-7876-3178-7
     1. Slavery–History–Sources. I. Knight, Judson.

HT863.S56 2000
306.3'62–dc21
                                         00-030265

Contents

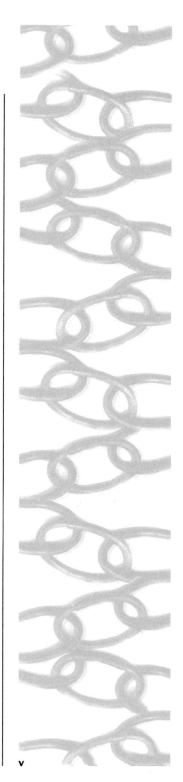

Reader's Guide

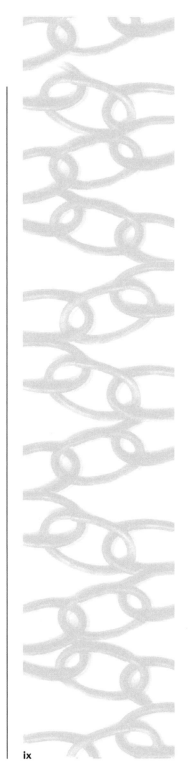

Slavery Throughout History: Primary Sources features twenty full or excerpted documents pertaining to the institution of slavery, from the Code of Hammurabi in ancient times to the rise of child laborers and sex slaves in Asia during the twentieth century. Some excerpts, such as Alexander Falconbridge's *An Account of the Slave Trade on the Coast of Africa,* relay the deplorable conditions slaves faced as they were transported from Africa to the New World, while other excerpts, including Aimé Bonifas's *Prisoner 20–801,* describe the determination people forced into slavery had to summon to become free.

Format

Slavery Throughout History: Primary Sources is divided into three chapters. Each chapter focuses on a specific time period in world slavery: Premodern Slavery (Ancient Times–A.D. 1500), Early Modern Slavery (1500–1900), and Late Modern Slavery (1900–Present). All three chapters open with an historical overview, followed by six to seven full-length or excerpted documents.

Each entry is divided into six sections:

- **Introductory material** places the document and its author in an historical context
- **Things to remember** offers readers important background information about the featured text
- **Excerpt** presents the document in its original format
- **What happened next** discusses the impact of the document on both the speaker and his or her audience
- **Did you know?** provides interesting facts about each document and its author
- **For more information** presents sources for further investigation into the documents and speakers

Additional Features

Many of the entries in *Slavery Throughout History: Primary Sources* contain sidebar boxes providing short biographies of the document's author or examining related excerpts, events, and issues, while sixty black-and-white illustrations help illuminate the text. Each excerpt is accompanied by a glossary running alongside the primary document that defines terms, people, and ideas discussed within the document. Also included within the volume is a timeline of important events and a subject index of the topics discussed in *Slavery Throughout History: Primary Sources.*

Comments and Suggestions

We welcome your comments on this work as well as your suggestions for topics to be featured in future editions of *Slavery Throughout History: Primary Sources.* Please write: Editors, *Slavery Throughout History: Primary Sources,* U•X•L, 27500 Drake Rd., Farmington Hills, MI 48331-3535; call toll-free: 1-800-877-4253; fax: 248-699-8097; or send e-mail via www.galegroup.com.

Timeline

1792–1750 B.C. Reign of **Hammurabi** in Babylonia. He created one of the world's first systems of laws, some of which dealt with the treatment of slaves.

334–322 B.C. Greek philosopher **Aristotle** writes most of his works, including *The Politics,* in which he explains his beliefs that some people are born to become slaves.

A.D. c. **70–c. 120** Career of **Plutarch**, Greco-Roman biographer and author of *Lives of the Noble Romans,* in which he describes the Gladiatorial War (73–71), a slave revolt led by Spartacus.

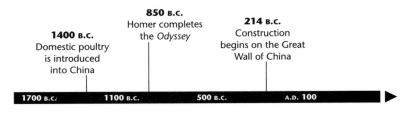

1400 B.C.
Domestic poultry is introduced into China

850 B.C.
Homer completes the *Odyssey*

214 B.C.
Construction begins on the Great Wall of China

1700 B.C.   1100 B.C.   500 B.C.   A.D. 100

549   **Fifth Council of Orleans,** like other Church councils during the Middle Ages, places regulations on European masters' treatment of their slaves and serfs.

570s   French historian **Gregory of Tours** writes the *History of the Franks.* The work explains that many masters did not follow the regulations the Church imposed for the treatment of slaves.

1388   Ottoman Turkish Sultan Murad I establishes the *Janissaries,* an elite group of slave soldiers. **James Ludlow's** work "The Tribute of Children" describes how many of these soldiers were enslaved as children.

1788   **Alexander Falconbridge,** a British surgeon who worked aboard a slave ship, writes *An Account of the Slave Trade on the Coast of Africa.*

1833   William Lloyd Garrison and others establish the **American Antislavery Society** (AAS) and issue its "Declaration of Sentiments" regarding slavery.

1838   Joseph Cinque leads the only successful slave-ship rebellion in U.S. history, aboard the *Amistad.* An earlier, but unsuccessful, revolt is described by slave trader **James Barbot** in "A Supplement to the Description of the Coasts of North and South Guinea."

1857   *Putnam's Monthly Magazine* publishes an article titled "A Slave's Story." Attributed only to "**Anonymous,**" the article describes the horrible life that a typical slave had to endure.

1862   President **Abraham Lincoln** issues the Emancipation Proclamation, which frees all slaves in the southern United States.

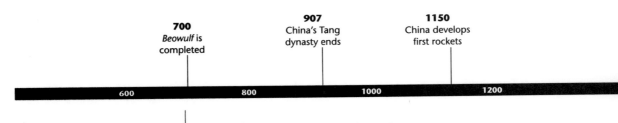

700
Beowulf is completed

907
China's Tang dynasty ends

1150
China develops first rockets

600   800   1000   1200

1865 The U.S. Congress ratifies, or passes, the **Thirteenth Amendment** to the United States Constitution, which outlaws slavery.

1868 The **Fourteenth Amendment** to the United States Constitution is adopted and establishes civil rights for freed slaves under state as well as federal law.

1870 The **Fifteenth Amendment** to the United States Constitution is ratified, extending the vote to all adult American males, regardless of race.

1940–45 French resistance fighter **Aimé Bonifas** is captured by Nazis and imprisoned in five different labor camps. He chronicled his experiences in his book, *Prisoner 20–801: A French National in the Nazi Labor Camps.*

1947 The **American Federation of Labor** publishes its statement "Free Labor vs. Slave Labor: Irrepressible Conflict."

1975 Communists in Vietnam, Cambodia, and Laos gain victory, and herd thousands of their people into "reeducation camps" (slave-labor camps). Roman Catholic priest **François Ponchaud** exposes these camps in his book *Cambodia: Year Zero.*

1990s Former "comfort women," like **Yun Turi,** begin to organize in an effort to petition the Japanese government for financial compensation and apologies.

Late 1990s Journalist **Huw Watkin** reports on the persistence of sex slavery in Asia; Indian scholar **Vijay Prashad** writes an article about the economic effect of child labor in places ranging from Southeast Asia to India to Brazil to the United States; and the **All Africa News Agency** reports that in Africa, old-fashioned chattel slavery remains a thriving business.

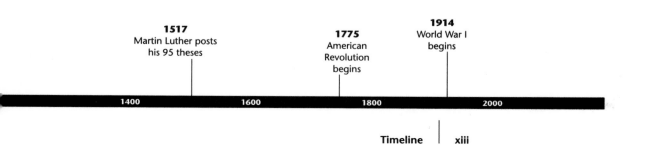

1517
Martin Luther posts
his 95 theses

1775
American
Revolution
begins

1914
World War I
begins

1400   1600   1800   2000

Premodern Slavery (Ancient Times–A.D. 1500)

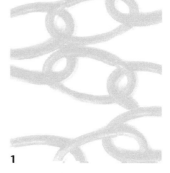

The term "premodern" encompasses both ancient times and the Middle Ages, also known as the medieval period, which lasted from about A.D. 500 to 1500. Although there were many changes during the premodern period, the way people lived then was so different from the way people live now it is useful to group these periods together.

In particular, the nature of slavery changed little in this period. During the modern era, slavery had racist overtones: white slaveholders claimed that they were racially superior to black Africans. However, in premodern times, slavery generally lacked this racial aspect. Certainly people, for the most part, considered slaves as inferior human beings; but this viewpoint was also influenced by ideas about nationality, social class, and even religion—not race.

Social class played a strong role in Babylonia, a highly developed ancient civilization in what is now Iraq. The greatest of Babylonia's early kings was **Hammurabi** (reigned 1792–c. 1750 B.C.), who created one of the world's first legal codes, or system of laws. The Code of Hammurabi provided important protections for weaker members of society, including widows and orphans, and even (to some extent) slaves.

According to the code, for instance, the child of a male slave and a free woman was free, and a slave could pass on money to his children after his death. Yet the code also revealed the extent to which social class determined the worth of a human being. If a rich man caused harm to a rich man, the punishment was serious, but not nearly as serious as the penalty if a slave harmed a rich man. By contrast, if a rich man harmed a slave, he only had to pay a fine to the slave's owner.

This seems unfair to modern observers, but not to ancient people, not even to an intelligent man such as the Greek philosopher **Aristotle** (384–322 B.C.) In Aristotle's view, which he explained in his *Politics,* it was clear that some people were born to be slaves, and others to be masters. This idea was related to the way the Greek people viewed the rest of the world: to them, the Greeks were the only civilized people, and all others were "barbarians." Hence it was fitting, in their minds, that the "barbarians" should serve the Greeks.

One such "barbarian" was the slave Spartacus, who was born in what is now Bulgaria. Spartacus lived almost three hundred years after Aristotle, and by that time Rome had taken Greece's place as the dominant power in Europe. To an even greater extent than the Greeks, Romans depended on slavery to sustain their civilization.

Like the Greeks, the Romans based their system of slavery on a belief that they had a right to enslave those people who were not Roman. Slavery was not based on race, since Rome's armies fought in all parts of the known world and slaves came from a variety of regions and racial backgrounds. What the enslaved people had in common was not skin color, but the fact that they came from countries less powerful than Rome.

In light of Greek and Roman attitudes toward slaves, it is interesting to read the sympathetic views of the Greek-born Roman historian **Plutarch** (A.D. c. 46–c. 119) regarding Spartacus. Plutarch described him as brave, honorable, and wise—certainly not traits most Greeks or Romans typically attributed to their slaves.

The Roman Empire in Western Europe would last until A.D. 476, but centuries of decline preceded its final collapse. In those centuries, slavery gradually gave way to a new system, which came to be known as serfdom. Serfs enjoyed slightly more freedom than slaves did, but there were far more of them. The growing institution of serfdom slowed Western Europe's development during the Middle Ages.

The Roman Catholic Church attempted to protect slaves and serfs from cruel masters by giving orders such as those handed down by the **Fifth Council of Orleans** in 549. However, as **Gregory of Tours** (538–594) later reported, the Church could not always keep the most wicked masters under control.

Although serfdom largely replaced the practice of slavery in Europe, traditional forms of slavery persisted in the Middle East and Africa. In addition, the Turks, who became the dominant force in the Middle East from about 1000 onward,

The ruins of the Roman coliseum where the Romans watched enslaved men like Spartacus fight each other or lions. Many of the great architectural structures of the Greek and Roman empires were built by slaves. *Reproduced by permission of AP/Wide World Photos, Inc.*

introduced a new concept: the slave-soldier. These were boys trained from youth for lives of hardship and service; yet unlike most other slaves, they could sometimes assume positions of great power. Particularly interesting were the Janissaries, described by **James M. Ludlow,** whose members were taken from the ranks of Christian men captured by the Muslim Turks.

Hammurabi

Excerpt from the Code of Hammurabi

Published in *Hammurabi, King of Babylonia:*
***The Letters and Inscriptions of Hammurabi, King of Babylon*, 1976**
Translated by L. W. King

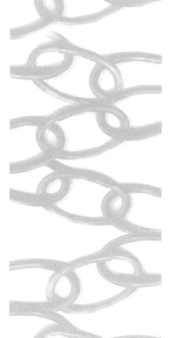

Hammurabi (1792 B.C.–?) established one of the world's first legal systems. As ruler of Babylonia (in what is now Iraq) during the 1700s B.C., Hammurabi conquered a large empire. To rule such a large and diverse area, he created a system of laws. Among the most notable features of this system are the protections it offered to the weak and vulnerable members of society, such as widows and orphans. On the other hand, it also established harsh punishments, and was the source of the idea "an eye for an eye," the belief that the punishment should be every bit as harsh as the crime itself.

The Code of Hammurabi consisted of 282 laws; thirty directly relate to the practice of slavery. These addressed various aspects of slavery, but there was one constant: the punishment depended on the status of the person harmed. In ancient Babylonia, there were three classes, or social groups: free men, who were the wealthiest and most powerful class; citizens or common men; and slaves. The greater the power of the person who committed a crime—and the lower the status of the victim—the smaller the penalty. The reverse was also true.

> If a slave say to his master: 'You are not my master,' if they convict him his master shall cut off his ear.

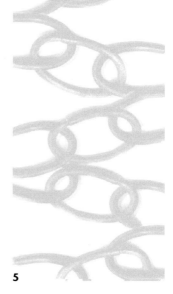

According to Laws 196 through 199, for instance, a free man who put out the eye of another free man would have his own eye removed. By contrast, if a free man did the same to a common man, he would merely have to pay a fee in silver; and if he poked out a slave's eye or killed the slave, he would have to pay half the slave's value, to the slave's owner and not to the slave.

Such aspects of Hammurabi's code may seem unfair to a modern person, but at the time it was an extremely generous set of laws. For instance, it established a number of provisions to protect women in situations such as divorce, which was highly unusual at a time when women had few rights. With regard to slaves, it at least provided a system of laws, which was much preferable to a system in which masters simply decided right and wrong on the spur of the moment.

Things to remember while reading

- The Code of Hammurabi begins with a short prologue, or introduction, and ends with an epilogue, or conclusion, that offers blessings for those who obey, and curses for those who do not. In between are 282 laws, of which approximately thirty (including the last one) involve slavery.

- Of the laws discussed, numbers 15 through 20 deal with runaway slaves; 117 through 119 with slaves sold to settle debts; 175 and 176 with children of a male slave and a free woman; and 217 through 224 with the punishments and rewards for a physician who harms or helps various societal groups, including slaves. Moreover, laws 226 and 227 relate to barbers, whose job it was to mark a slave prior to sale, and laws 280 and 281 address slaves stolen and sold in another country. The last of Hammurabi's laws dictates a severe punishment for a slave who verbally defies his master.

- Despite the many harsh laws regarding slaves, a number of provisions in Hammurabi's code are quite generous—particularly by the standards of the day. For example, law 119 addresses situations in which an owner is unable to pay off his debts and sells a female slave with whom he

An illustration of ancient
Babylonia where Hammurabi
dispensed his code.
*Reproduced by permission of
Archive Photos, Inc.*

has fathered children. Recognizing the difficulty this would pose for the slave, and the significance of the bond created by children, the code provides that the owner must later purchase the slave's freedom. Also notable are the provisions in numbers 175 and 176, whereby the children of a slave and a free woman are free, and the master of a deceased slave with children has a right to no more than half of the slave's property.

- As was typical of ancient documents, these laws primarily address males—whether free man, common man, or slave. Hammurabi's code was unusual in referring to women at all; more often, ancient laws simply ignored them.

The Code of Hammurabi

...15. If any one take a male or female slave of the court, or a male or female slave of a freed man, outside the city gates, he shall be put to death.

16. If any one receive into his house a runaway male or female slave of the court, or of a freedman, and does not bring it out at the public proclamation of the **major domus**, the master of the house shall be put to death.

17. If any one find runaway male or female slaves in the open country and bring them to their masters, the master of the slaves shall pay him two **shekels** of silver.

18. If the slave will not give the name of the master, the finder shall bring him to the palace; a further investigation must follow, and the slave shall be returned to his master.

19. If he [the person who found the runaway slave or slaves] hold the slaves in his house, and they are caught there, he shall be put to death.

20. If the slave that he caught run away from him, then shall he swear to the owners of the slave [that he did not assist the slave's escape], and he is free of all blame.

...117. If any one fail **to meet a claim for debt**, and sell himself, his wife, his son, and daughter for money or give them away to forced labor: they shall work for three years in the house of the man who bought them, or the **proprietor**, and in the fourth year they shall be set free.

118. If he [slaveholder] give a male or female slave away for forced labor, and the merchant **sublease** them, or sell them for money, no objection can be raised [by the man who originally owned the slaves].

119. If any one fail to meet a claim for debt, and he sell the maid servant who has borne him children, for money, the money which the merchant [i.e. the buyer] has paid shall [later] be repaid to him by the owner of the slave and she shall be freed.

...175. If a **State slave** or the slave of a freed man marry the daughter of a free man, and children are born, the master of the

Major domus: A leading official of the palace, who served as spokesman for the king.

Shekels: Gold coins.

To meet a claim for debt: To pay off one's debts.

Proprietor: Someone who operates an establishment—in this case, the house of the master.

Sublease: An arrangement in which a person who is renting something (for instance, a residence) in turn rents it to another person, while retaining the contract for the original rent.

State slave: A slave owned by the government rather than by a private household.

Dowry: The wealth that a bride brings to her marriage.

Found: Establish.

Means: Wealth.

Tumor: A diseased growth.

Incision: Cut.

Soft part: Something that is not bone.

slave shall have no right to enslave the children of the free.

176. If, however, a State slave or the slave of a freed man marry a [free] man's daughter, and after he marries her she bring a **dowry** from a father's house, if then they both enjoy it and **found** a household, and accumulate **means**, if then the slave die, then she who was free born may take her dowry, and all that her husband and she had earned; she shall divide them into two parts, one-half the master for the slave shall take, and the other half shall the free-born woman take for her children. If the free-born woman had no gift [i.e. dowry] she shall take all that her husband and she had earned and divide it into two parts; and the master of the slave shall take one-half and she shall take the other for her children.

...215. If a physician ... open a **tumor** [over the eye] with an operating knife, and saves the eye, he shall receive ten shekels in money.

216. If the patient be a freed man, he receives five shekels.

217. If he be the slave of some one, his owner shall give the physician two shekels.

218. If a physician make a large **incision** with the operating knife, and kill him [freed man], or open a tumor with the operating knife, and cut out the eye, his hands shall be cut off.

219. If a physician make a large incision in the slave of a freed man, and kill him, he shall replace the slave with another slave.

...221. If a physician heal the broken bone or diseased **soft part** of a man, the patient shall pay the physician five shekels in money.

222. If he were a freed man he shall pay three shekels.

223. If he were a slave his owner shall pay the physician two shekels.

Engraved into this stone stele is Hammurabi's code, as well as an image of Hammurabi giving his subjects this code.
Reproduced by permission of Corbis-Bettmann.

224. If a veterinary surgeon perform a serious operation on an ass or an ox, and cure it, the owner shall pay the surgeon one-sixth of a shekel as a fee.

*...226. If a barber, without the knowledge of his master, **cut the sign of a slave** on a slave not to be sold, the hands of this barber shall be cut off.*

*227. If any one **deceive** a barber, and have him mark a slave not for sale with the sign of a slave, he shall be put to death, and buried in his house. The barber shall swear: "I did not mark him **wittingly**," and shall be guiltless.*

...280. If while in a foreign country a man buy a male or female slave belonging to another of his own country; if when he return home the owner of the male or female slave recognize it: if the male or female slave be a native of the country, he shall give them back without any money.

*281. If they are from another country, the buyer shall declare the amount of money paid **therefor** to the merchant, and keep the male or female slave.*

282. If a slave say to his master: "You are not my master," if they convict him his master shall cut off his ear....

What happened next...

Hammurabi died in approximately 1750 B.C., and with him died the power and glory of his reign. It would be many centuries before another powerful king emerged in Babylonia; indeed, the country entered a period of decline soon after his death, and the next thousand years would be characterized by a series of invasions from all sides.

Hammurabi's son fought off a number of attacks from invading peoples, among them the Hittites from Asia Minor (modern-day Turkey). In 1600 B.C. the Hittites destroyed Babylonia. Five years later, a group called the Kassites seized control of the region and held it for three centuries.

In the turmoil that followed Hammurabi's death, it is not surprising that his laws held little influence. In fact there

Hammurabi

Babylonia was an ancient kingdom in Mesopotamia, in present-day Iraq. It is remembered for its splendid capital city, Babylon, and for its many achievements in areas ranging from astronomy (the study of the stars) to architecture to law. Its two most famous rulers were Nebuchadnezzar II (reigned c. 630–562 B.C.), and—more than a thousand years before him—Hammurabi.

The period from 3000 to 1792 B.C. is referred to by historians as "Old Babylonia," an era that preceded the greatest achievements of Babylonian civilization. The beginning of Hammurabi's forty-two-year reign in 1792 marked the opening chapter of a new and glorious (though brief) phase in Babylonia's history.

Hammurabi quickly distinguished himself as a leader by defeating a neighboring king who tried to take over Isin, an important city in the region. During the decades that followed, Hammurabi defeated all of the kings in all of the surrounding areas. Eventually his empire stretched from the southern part of modern-day Iraq to the Mediterranean Sea far in the west.

During his long reign, Hammurabi built many ziggurats, or temple towers. Historians believe that the Tower of Babel, described in the Old Testament of the Bible, may have been constructed under his leadership. He supervised numerous other building projects, including the construction of fortifications, or defensive walls, around the city of Babylon.

However, Hammurabi's greatest achievement was his legal system. Though many of those laws may seem unfair to a modern person, at the time they represented a great step for justice. In particular, the Code of Hammurabi provided protections for people who usually had none, including widows, orphans, and slaves.

is no evidence that his legal code was ever enforced in the years that followed his reign. Ultimately, however, the Code of Hammurabi would be highly influential: though it was not the first legal code in history, it is the first known code. As such, it provides much insight into how legal systems work and develop.

Did you know...

- Strictly speaking, the Code of Hammurabi is not a true code of law because it only added to already existing laws. Nonetheless, it is the oldest statement of laws known in the world and formed the basis for later legal systems.

- Among the issues dealt with in the Code of Hammurabi are personal property, real estate, business, trade, agriculture, marriage, inheritances, adoption, contracts, and leases.

- The code was carved into a large stele, or stone pillar, with an illustration of Hammurabi receiving the laws from Babylonia's gods.

- More than ten percent of Hammurabi's code, specifically, the laws between number 65 and number 100, is missing.

For more information

Books

King, L. W., trans. *Hammurabi, King of Babylonia: The Letters and Inscriptions of Hammurabi, King of Babylon.* New York: AMS Press, 1976.

Sources

Books

Baumann, Hans. *In the Land of Ur: The Discovery of Ancient Mesopotamia.* Translated by Stella Humphreys. New York: Pantheon, 1969.

Landau, Elaine. *The Babylonians.* Brookfield, Conn.: Millbrook Press, 1997.

Malam, John. *Mesopotamia and the Fertile Crescent: 10,000 to 539 B.C.* Austin, Tex.: Raintree Steck-Vaughn, 1999.

Other

"Ancient History Sourcebook: Code of Hammurabi, c. 1780 BCE." *Ancient History Sourcebook.* http://www.fordham.edu/halsall/ancient/hamcode.html (accessed on January 17, 2000).

"Hammurabi's Code of Laws (1780 BC)." *World Wide Legal Information Association.* http://www.wwlia.org/hamm1.htm (accessed on January 17, 2000.)

"You Be the Judge on Hammurabi's Code." http://members.xoom.com/_XMCM/PMartin/hammurabicodeoflaw.htm (accessed on January 17, 2000).

Aristotle

Excerpt from **The Politics of Aristotle**
Published in *The Politics of Aristotle,* **1900**

Although ancient Greece introduced the concept of democracy (a government ruled by its citizens), Greek society was also highly dependent on slave labor. In fact, only a small group of people in ancient Greece—the citizens—actually enjoyed the benefits of democracy, such as the opportunity to vote. The citizens were made up of free Greek males. Women were forbidden to vote, as were foreigners. So, too, was the largest group in Greek society: slaves.

Ancient Greece was never a single nation, but a collection of several hundred self-governing city-states. These tiny districts functioned as separate countries, but tended to follow the lead of the most important city-states, particularly Athens and Sparta. Sparta was a military dictatorship, an extremely harsh, organized system ruled by a small group. Not surprisingly, the vast majority of its people were slaves. Yet even Athens, the birthplace of democracy and indeed of Western civilization, was hugely dependent on slave labor.

Even a highly intelligent, educated Athenian citizen could support the cause of freedom for some people and accept the concept of slavery. Such was the case with Aristotle

> For that some should rule and others be ruled is a thing not only necessary, but expedient....

The ruins of the Parthenon in Athens, Greece. The Parthenon was a temple built by slaves to the goddess Athena.
Photograph by Susan D. Rock. Reproduced by permission.

(384–322 B.C.), who is considered one of the greatest Greek philosophers. (Philosophers are concerned with the essential nature of reality, and in the course of their study they examine different aspects of life.) Aristotle's interests were extremely wide-ranging, and he wrote hundreds of books on subjects exploring such topics as science, music, and politics.

Many aspects of Aristotle's thinking had a liberating effect: his writings helped scientists, for instance, reach a better understanding of how they knew what they knew. Yet in his discussion of slavery from the *Politics,* Aristotle revealed himself as a man tied to his time and place. He lived in a world built by slavery, and he was not inclined to question it.

Things to remember while reading

- Although many of the ideas expressed by Aristotle in this passage are offensive to a modern reader, it is important to remember the time and place in which he was writing. The Greeks looked down on other societies and considered their own, which had been built on the backs of slaves, superior to all others. Aristotle was among the wisest men who ever lived, and did much to advance the cause of human freedom; yet when it came to the subject of slavery he was (like most people) unable to challenge the beliefs of his time.

- A number of the ideas expressed in this passage reflects Aristotle's Greek heritage. The ancient Greeks tended to regard anyone who was not Greek as a barbarian, or uncivilized person; and they viewed women as vastly inferior to men. They also placed little value on mercy or compassion.

- Like his teacher Plato, Aristotle regarded the ability to think as the most important qualification for a person. He also believed that people's destinies were already determined for them. He wrote that free people were superior to slaves, using as justification the fact that free people work with their minds and slaves with their bodies. Yet one might object that free people think, and slaves labor, because in either case, that is their job. To this Aristotle would say that some people are born to be slaves and others to be free.

The Politics of Aristotle

*Let us first speak of master and slave, looking to the needs of practical life and also seeking to attain some better theory of their relation than exists at present.... Property is a part of the household, and the art of acquiring property is a part of the art of managing the household; for no man can live well, or indeed live at all, unless he be provided with **necessaries** And so, in the arrangement of the family, a slave is a living possession, and property a number of such instruments; and the slave is himself an instrument which takes **precedence** of all other instruments.... The master is only the master of the slave; he does not belong to him, whereas the slave is not only the slave of his master, but wholly belongs to him. Hence we see*

Necessaries: Things necessary to living.

Precedence of...: Importance over....

*what is the nature and **office** of a slave; he who is by nature not his own but another's man, is by nature a slave; and he may be said to be another's man who, being a human being, is also a possession. And a possession may be defined as an **instrument of action**, separable from the possessor.*

*But is there any one thus intended by nature to be a slave, and for whom such a condition is **expedient** and right, or rather is not all slavery a violation of nature? There is no difficulty in answering this question, on grounds both of reason and of fact. For that some should rule and others be ruled is a thing not only necessary, but expedient; from the hour of their birth, some are marked out for **subjection**, others for rule.... Again, the male is by nature superior, and the female inferior; and the one rules, and the other is ruled; this principle, of necessity, extends to all mankind.*

*Where then there is such a difference as that between soul and body, or between men and animals (as in the case of those whose business is to use their body, and who can do nothing better), the lower sort are by nature slaves, and it is better for them as for all inferiors that they should be under the rule of a master. For he who can be, and therefore is, another's [property] and he who participates in **rational principle** enough to **apprehend**, but not to have, such a principle, is a slave by nature. Whereas the lower animals cannot even apprehend a principle; they obey their instincts. And indeed the use made of slaves and of tame animals is not very different; for both with their bodies minister to the needs of life. Nature **would like to** distinguish between the bodies of freemen and slaves, making the one strong for **servile** labor, the other upright, and although useless for such services, useful for political life in the arts both of war and peace. But the opposite often happens—that some have the souls and others have the bodies of free men. And doubtless if men differed from one another in the mere forms of their bodies as much as the statues of the gods do from men, all would acknowledge that the inferior class should be slaves of the superior. It is clear, then, that some men are by nature free, and others slaves, and that for these latter slavery is both expedient and right.*

*There is a slave or slavery by law as well as by nature. The law of which I speak is a sort of **convention**—the law by which whatever is taken in war is supposed to belong to the victors. But this right many **jurists impeach**, as they would an **orator** who brought forward an **unconstitutional measure**: they detest the notion that, because one man has the power of doing violence and is superior in brute*

Office: function

Instrument of action: A tool.

Expedient: Suitable or proper.

Subjection: slavery.

Rational principle: Intelligent thought.

Apprehend: Understand.

Would like to: Should.

Servile: Slavelike.

Convention: Widely accepted rule.

Jurists: Lawyers.

Impeach: Oppose.

Orator: Speaker.

Unconstitutional measure: A law which violates existing laws.

Virtue: Rightness.

Means: Power.

Plausibility: Believability.

Hellenes: Greeks.

strength, another shall be his slave and subject. Even among philosophers there is a difference of opinion. The origin of the dispute, and what makes the views invade each other's territory, is as follows: in some sense **virtue**, when furnished with **means**, has actually the greatest power of exercising force; and as superior power is only found where there is superior excellence of some kind, power seems to imply virtue, and the dispute to be simply one about justice (for it is due to one party identifying justice with goodwill while the other identifies it with the mere rule of the stronger). If these views are thus set out separately, the other views have no force or **plausibility** against the view that the superior in virtue ought to rule, or be master.

Others, clinging, as they think, simply to a principle of justice (for law and custom are a sort of justice), assume that slavery in accordance with the custom of war is justified by law, but at the same moment they deny this. For what if the cause of the war be unjust? And again, no one would ever say he is a slave who is unworthy to be a slave. Were this the case, men of the highest rank would be slaves and the children of slaves if they or their parents chance to have been taken captive and sold. Wherefore **Hellenes** do not like to call Hellenes slaves, but confine the term to **barbarians**. Yet, in using this language, they really mean the natural slave of whom we spoke at first; for it must be admitted that some are slaves everywhere, others nowhere. The same principle applies to **nobility**. Hellenes regard themselves as noble everywhere, and not only in their own country, but they deem the barbarians noble only when at home, thereby implying that there are two sorts of nobility and freedom, the one **absolute**, the other **relative**.

Greek philosopher Aristotle believed that some people were born to be slaves.
Reproduced by permission of Corbis-Bettmann.

Barbarians: Uncivilized people; the Greeks called all non-Greeks "barbarians."

Nobility: The quality of being noble, or greater than others.

Absolute: Fixed and unchanging.

Relative: Dependent on outside factors; the opposite of absolute.

Aristotle

Along with his teacher Plato and Plato's teacher Socrates, Aristotle was one of the three most influential philosophers of ancient Greece. Aristotle's interests were extremely broad. He wrote about subjects as diverse as biology, drama, and politics.

Born in the town of Stagira, Aristotle came from the region of Macedonia to the north of Greece, where his father served as court physician to the Macedonian king. At age seventeen, Aristotle went to Athens, cultural center of Greece, to study under the renowned philosopher Plato. For twenty years, he remained at Plato's school—known as the Academy—during which time he proved to be the great philosopher's most outstanding pupil. Later, however, he would reject most of Plato's ideas and develop an entirely independent system of thought.

Aristotle married at age forty; soon afterward, his father-in-law was killed. Later, his wife Pythias died during childbirth. It was after these traumatic events that Aristotle received an intriguing offer from King Philip of Macedonia, who asked him to come to the Macedonian court to tutor his teenage son Alexander—who was destined to become known as Alexander the Great (356–323 B.C.).

Aristotle tutored Alexander for four years, then served King Philip in a number of other ways. In 334 B.C., as Alexander began to win a series of wars that would make him the greatest conqueror in history, Aristotle opened a school of his own in Athens, the Lyceum. During the years that followed, the Lyceum would welcome a wide variety of students (in contrast to Plato's upper-class Academy). Aristotle would put his pupils to work assisting him in a wide array of research projects.

Also in 334 B.C., Aristotle began writing down his ideas. In the next twelve years, he produced some four hundred books, of which only forty survive. In 323 B.C., he received word that Alexander had died, and fearing an anti-Macedonian reaction in Athens, he left the city. A year later he died in the city of Chalcis on a nearby island.

What happened next...

Ancient Greece flourished in spite of its slave system; indeed, one might say it flourished in part *because of* slavery, which allowed free men the time and leisure to undertake some of the most brilliant writing and thinking in human history. Yet by Aristotle's time, the sun was setting on Greece's glory.

In the mid-330s B.C., Greece was under the control of Alexander the Great, Aristotle's old pupil. Although Alexander considered himself Greek, he was really a Macedonian, and the Greeks viewed him as an outsider. Thus the fact that he was able to bring all of Greece under his control signaled the weakening of Athens and the other city-states. As it turned out, Alexander's campaign of conquest, which resulted in an empire that stretched from Italy to India, was Greece's last hurrah.

During the two centuries that followed, Greek civilization, including its ideas about slavery, spread throughout the Mediterranean region. By then Rome was becoming an empire, however, and in 146 B.C. it added Greece to its territories. Romans had long admired and imitated Greek civilization, and as a result, Rome was destined to become a society dependent on the institution of slavery, just like Greece.

Did you know...

- A wealthy household in ancient Greece typically owned between ten and twenty slaves.

- The going rate for a healthy slave in ancient Greece was ten *minae,* or about $180.00. Old or otherwise undesirable slaves, including ones who refused to work, could sell for as little as 0.5 minae, or $9.00.

- Surprisingly, Athens's police force was made up primarily of slaves. It is hard to imagine how the Athenians could have prevented a slave revolt if firearms had existed in ancient times.

For more information

Books

Aristotle. *The Politics of Aristotle.* Translated by Benjamin Jowett. New York: Colonial Press, 1900.

Sources

Books

Furan, Rodney. *Twelve Great Philosophers.* Mankato, Minn.: Oddo Publishing, 1968.

Illustrated Introduction to Philosophy. New York: DK Publishing, Inc., 1998.

Other

"Ancient History Sourcebook: Documents on Greek Slavery, c. 750–330 BCE." *Ancient History Sourcebook.* http://www.fordham.edu/halsall/ancient/greek-slaves.html (accessed on January 13, 2000).

"Slavery in Ancient Greece." http://www.adm.pdx.edu/user/sinq/greekciv/sport/kirsten.html (accessed on January 18, 2000).

Plutarch

Excerpt from Lives of the Noble Romans
Published in *Lives of the Noble Romans*, 1959

Few societies in history have been as dependent on slavery as ancient Rome. In fact, Romans lived in terror of a slave uprising; in 73 B.C., their worst fears were realized when a slave named Spartacus led a slave revolt. Over the course of two years, approximately 120,000 slaves fought the Roman forces throughout Italy before finally being defeated in 71 B.C.

This conflict is known as the Gladiatorial War, because Spartacus and the others who began it were gladiators, or warriors who fought to their deaths in a ring while cheering spectators watched. Slaves like Spartacus were trained to be gladiators at a center run by Lentulus Batiates, in the southern Italian city of Capua.

Spartacus came from Thrace, which was located in the area that is present-day Bulgaria. Many of the other slaves at the school were either Thracians or Gauls. Gaul was the Roman term for the Celts, a tribal group that lived in areas to the north of Italy.

The gladiators of Capua may have started the revolt, but soon slaves from all over Italy joined the uprising. The senate, Rome's governing body, first appointed Clodius to

"Spartacus was chief, a Thracian of one of the nomad tribes, and a man not only of high spirit and valiant, but in understanding, also, and in gentleness superior to his condition...."

The gladiator Spartacus led one of the most famous slave revolts of the Roman Empire.
Sculpture by Vinnie Ream Hoxie. Courtesy of The Library of Congress.

lead the army against the slaves. Clodius was a praetor, an official whose powers were similar to that of a judge. (In Rome, every governmental figure also doubled as a military commander.) However, as reported by the Greek historian Plutarch (A.D. c. 46–119), in his *Lives of the Noble Romans,* Clodius was unable to defeat the rebels.

Italy is a peninsula (a body of land surrounded on three sides by water), and over the course of the war, the rebels moved up and down the country. At one point they reached the Alps, the high mountains that form Italy's northern border. From there, Spartacus hoped that they would all return to their homeland. His army overruled him and continued fighting. Rome dispatched two consuls, the top officials in the Roman government, against the rebel, but still the slaves kept fighting. It was then that Crassus (c. 115–53 B.C.) appeared on the scene.

Rumored to be the wealthiest man in Rome at the time, Crassus hoped that by defeating the slaves, he also could become the most powerful man as well. Soon, however, the slaves won a victory over his lieutenant Mummius at Picenum in eastern Italy. The rebels moved on to Lucania in the south, and from there, Spartacus hoped they could escape to Sicily, a large island off the southwestern tip of Italy. To that end, he paid a group of pirates from Cilicia in Asia Minor (modern-day Turkey) for the use of their ships. The pirates, however, simply took the slaves' money and left them stranded.

The fighting continued. Crassus resolved to end the revolt when he learned that Pompey (106–48 B.C.), one of Rome's most distinguished generals, was on his way. He knew that Pompey might very well defeat the slaves and gain all the glory for himself; thus Plutarch noted that Crassus was "eager to fight a decisive [conclusive] battle."

Things to remember while reading

- The following excerpt is condensed from the chapter on Crassus in *Lives of the Noble Romans,* which was written by Plutarch. Among the parts omitted are accounts of the slaves' battles with several generals after the defeat of Clodius and before the appointment of Crassus. Also omitted are further details of the rebel army's battles with Crassus after their betrayal by the Cilician pirates and before the final showdown in Lucania.

- Because he was Greek, some of Plutarch's comments reflect his Greek viewpoint. The Greeks considered the Thracians—and indeed anyone who was not Greek—to be barbarians, or uncivilized people; therefore, by noting that Spartacus was "more of a Grecian than the people of his country usually are," Plutarch was paying him high praise.

- As with Rome, the economy of Greece was dependent on slavery, yet Plutarch showed a degree of sympathy with the slaves when he wrote that they were put in the position of becoming gladiators "not for any fault by them committed," i.e., through no fault of their own. He also suggested that the fact that Spartacus was a slave did not make him less of a human being; hence his comment that the rebel leader was "in gentleness [honorable nature] superior to his condition."

- The translator of the text, English poet John Dryden (1631–1700), used British spellings such as "honour."

Plutarch

Although his writing has provided historians with valuable information concerning the ancient world, Plutarch was not, strictly speaking, a historian. Rather, he was a biographer of notable figures in Greece and Rome. He published these short biographies in several collections, such as *Lives of the Noble Romans* and *Parallel Lives.* The latter collection presented paired biographies of Greek and Roman figures, establishing links between men separated by time and geography. Plutarch's work is highly readable, and offers insights on a number of key figures from ancient times.

Long before Plutarch's time, Greece had fallen under the control of the Roman Empire. Nonetheless, the Greeks, not to mention the Romans themselves, looked to Athens for cultural leadership. Therefore as a young man, Plutarch left his home in Chaeronea, in central Greece, to study in Athens under a teacher named Ammonius. He later traveled throughout the known world, performing research for his writings. He spent his final years in Chaeronea.

The word "waggon" is a British variation on "wagon."

Insurrection: Armed uprising.

Gladiators: Warriors who fought in a ring—usually until one of them died—while spectators watched.

Devastation: Destruction.

Lives of the Noble Romans

*The **insurrection** of the **gladiators** and the **devastation** of Italy, commonly called the war of Spartacus, began upon this occasion. One Lentulus Batiates trained up a great many gladiators in Capua, most of them Gauls and Thracians, who, not for any fault by them committed, but simply through the cruelty of their master, were kept in confinement for this object of fighting one with another. Two hundred of these formed a plan to escape, but being discovered, those of them who became aware of it in time to **anticipate their master**, being seventy-eight, got out of a cook's shop chopping-knives and **spits**, and made their way through the city, and lighting by the way on several waggons that were carrying gladiators' arms to another city, they seized upon them and armed themselves. And seizing upon a defensible place, they chose three captains, of whom Spartacus was chief, a Thracian of one of the nomad tribes, and a man not only of high spirit and **valiant**, but in understanding, also, and in gentleness superior to his condition, and more of a Grecian than the people of his country usually are. When he first came to be sold at Rome, they say a snake coiled itself upon his face as he lay asleep, and his wife ... a kind of prophetess ... declared that it was a sign **portending** great and **formidable** power to him **with no happy event**.*

*First, then, **routing** those that came out of Capua against them, and thus **procuring** a quantity of proper soldiers' arms, they gladly threw away their own as **barbarous** and dishonourable. Afterwards Clodius, the **praetor**, took the command against them with a body of three thousand men from Rome, and **besieged** them within a mountain, accessible only by one narrow and difficult passage, which Clodius kept guarded, **encompassed** on all* other sides with steep and slippery **precipices**. Upon the top, however, grew a great many wild vines, and cutting down as many of their boughs as they had need of, they [the slaves] twisted them into strong ladders long enough to reach from **thence** to the bottom, by which, without any danger, they got down all but one, who stayed there to throw them down their arms, and after this succeeded in saving himself.... Several also, of the shepherds and herdsmen that were there, stout and nimble fellows, revolted over to them [the slaves' side], to some of whom they gave complete arms, and made use of others as scouts and light-armed soldiers. ...[Spartacus] began to be **great and terrible**; but wisely considering that he was not to expect to match the force of the empire, he marched his army towards the Alps, intending, when he had passed them, that every man should go to his own home, some to Thrace, some to Gaul. But they, grown confident in their numbers, and puffed up with their success, would give no obedience to him, but went about and **ravaged** Italy; so that now the senate was not only moved at the **indignity** and **baseness**, both of the enemy and of the insurrection, but, looking upon it as a matter of alarm and of dangerous consequence sent out both the **consuls** to it, as to a great and difficult enterprise....

...[Later,] they appointed Crassus general of the war, and a great many of the nobility went volunteers with him, partly out of friendship, and partly **to get honour**. He stayed himself on the borders of Picenum, expecting Spartacus would come that way, and sent his lieutenant, Mummius, with two **legions**, to wheel about and observe the enemy's motions, but upon no account to **engage or skirmish**. But he [Mummius], upon the first opportunity, joined battle, and was routed, having a great many of his men slain, and a great many only saving their lives with the loss of their arms. Crassus **rebuked** Mummius severely, and arming the soldiers again ... he led them against the enemy; but Spartacus retreated through Lucania toward the sea, and in the straits meeting with some Cilician pirate ships, he had thoughts of attempting Sicily, where, by landing two thousand men, he hoped to rekindle the war of the slaves, which was but lately extinguished, and seemed to need but little fuel to set it burning again. But after the pirates had struck a bargain with him, and received his **earnest**, they deceived him and sailed away....

...[N]ews was already brought that Pompey was **at hand**; and people began to talk openly that the honour of this war was

Anticipate their master: Form a plan to avoid punishment and escape from their master.

Spits: Pointed rods for holding meat over a fire.

Valiant: Brave.

Portending: Indicating or foretelling.

Formidable: Impressive.

With no happy event: In other words, "Without a happy ending."

Routing: Dispersing.

Procuring: Gaining possession of.

Barbarous: Uncivilized.

Praetor: A high Roman official, similar to that of a judge but also possessing a military command.

Besieged: Attacked.

Encompassed: Surrounded.

Precipices: Steep overhangs, or cliffs.

Thence: In this case, the top of the cliff.

*reserved to him, who would come and at once oblige the enemy to fight and put an end to the war. Crassus, therefore, eager to fight a **decisive** battle, encamped very near the enemy, and began to make **lines of circumvallation**; but the slaves made a **sally** and attacked the **pioneers**. As fresh supplies came in on either side, Spartacus, seeing there was no avoiding it, set all his army **in array**; and when his horse was brought him, he drew out his sword and killed him, saying, if he **got the day** he should have a great many better horses of the enemies', and if he lost it he should have no need of this. And so making directly towards Crassus himself, through the midst of arms and wounds, he missed him, but **slew** two **centurions** that fell upon him together. At last being deserted by those that were about him, he himself stood his ground, and, surrounded by the enemy, bravely defending himself, was cut in pieces....*

What happened next...

Spartacus's death in battle was not only a heroic act, but in light of what happened to the slaves after their defeat by Crassus's army, it was probably also a wise choice. The soldiers took some six thousand rebel slaves prisoner and subjected them to a form of punishment common in Rome at that time: crucifixion. They hung their bodies at intervals of one hundred paces along the Appian Way between Capua to Rome, a distance of some ninety miles. To the remaining slaves in Rome, the message was clear: any further revolt would be met with the harshest punishment possible.

The Gladiatorial War set in motion a chain of events that made it one of the most significant, if not well-known, conflicts in history. Having established himself as one of the most powerful men in Rome, Crassus, along with Pompey and Julius Caesar (100–44 B.C.), formed a triumvirate, or government of three. Though Rome still called itself a republic—meaning that it was governed by elected officials—in fact all power rested in the hands of the three men that formed the triumvirate.

Slavery in Rome did not so much end as it faded away. Once Rome quit making overseas conquests in the A.D. 100s, it no longer had a source for slaves. In addition, as the Roman economy declined, few people could afford to keep slaves. The feudal system, under which powerful landowners virtually owned poor farmers (called serfs), took the place of slavery during the Middle Ages (c. 500–1500).

A drawing showing the death of Spartacus.
Drawing by H. Vogel. Reproduced by permission of Corbis-Bettmann.

Did you know...

- The Romans called their slaves "speaking tools," indicating that they considered them less than human.

- In the 1960 film *Spartacus,* Kirk Douglas played the title role, with Laurence Olivier as Crassus and Peter Ustinov as Lentulus Batiates. The director was Stanley Kubrick, acclaimed for a number of later films such as *2001: A Space Odyssey* (1968). The screenwriters took some liberties with history, adding a love affair between Spartacus (who in their version was unmarried) and a slave girl named Virgilia, played by Jean Simmons.

- The name of Spartacus has remained a powerful symbol for armies of poor and oppressed people intent on overthrowing the existing political system. In 1919 a group of rebels called the Spartacus League led an unsuccessful uprising in Germany.

For more information

Books

Plutarch. *Lives of the Noble Romans.* Translated by John Dryden, edited by Edmund Fuller. New York: Dell Publishing, 1959, pp. 152-57.

Sources

Books

Hadas, Moses. *Imperial Rome.* New York: Time-Life Books, 1965.

Houghton, Eric. *They Marched with Spartacus.* New York: McGraw-Hill, 1963.

Other

"Ancient History Sourcebook: Slavery in the Roman Republic." http://www.fordham.edu/halsall/ancient/slavery-romrep1.html (accessed on December 1, 1999).

Spartacus (motion picture). Universal Studios Home Video, 1960.

The Fifth Council of Orleans

Excerpt from Laws Concerning Slaves and Freedmen
Published in *A Sourcebook for Medieval Economic History*, 1936
Edited by Roy C. Cave and Herbert H. Coulson

Gregory of Tours

Excerpt from History of the Franks
Published in *A Sourcebook for Medieval Economic History*, 1936
Edited by Roy C. Cave and Herbert H. Coulson

In the Middle Ages, the period between about A.D. 500 and 1500, the issue of slavery in Europe became more confusing. During this period, only about ten percent of the people in Europe were slaves—but another forty percent were serfs, poor farmers who enjoyed just a bit more freedom than actual slaves.

The dominant political force in Europe during the Middle Ages was the Roman Catholic Church, whose leadership passed laws that applied to the population as a whole, just like the laws of a government. Much of this activity took place at church councils, or conferences. It was at these events that bishops (high-ranking priests with authority over the believers in a given region) considered a number of matters. One such council was held in the French city of Orleans in 549.

The Fifth Council of Orleans, as it was called, addressed a number of issues, including the treatment of runaway slaves and serfs. The council urged masters to be merciful to runaway slaves, but as Catholic bishop and historian Gregory of Tours (538–594) reported a quarter-century later, many masters simply ignored the recommendations of the Church.

But concerning slaves, who flee for refuge to the church on account of any offense, we decree that it should be observed that they be sent away certain of forgiveness, just as is acknowledged to have been written in ancient laws....

From the Laws Concerning Slaves and Freedmen

Things to remember while reading

- The Fifth Council of Orleans was a group of bishops, or church leaders, making policy for the Church—and because of the great power of the Roman Catholic Church, all of Europe.

- As the members of the Council of Orleans noted, the Church offered a safe haven, and in some cases freedom, to slaves. A runaway slave could be certain that the Church would forgive him or her for running away; the Church also encouraged slaveholders to be forgiving as well. On the other hand, Church leaders did not want to make the Church seem "as if it had appeared desirous of retaining the [runaway] slave," nor did they want to defy existing laws. Hence they made an exception "for those faults for which the laws ordered revocation of the liberties conferred on slaves": thus if a slave had committed a serious crime in the course of running away, there was nothing the Church could do to protect him or her.

- In general, however, the Church was interested in limiting slavery. To this end, the council members encouraged free men who sold themselves into bondage to buy themselves out of slavery as soon as possible: "if they can find the price, as much as was given for them, when the price is given, they shall be restored to their former status without delay." Like Hammurabi (see entry), the council decreed, or ruled, that the children of a slave and a free person were free. In dealing with non-Christian slaveholders, the council suggested that a Christian should guarantee the protection of the slave, because a Christian would be kept in line by his fear of the Church's authority.

- Gregory indicated that the cruel slaveholder Rauching punished a slave who, "as was customary ... held a burning candle before him at dinner." Presumably the slave was only providing the master with light, and perhaps he or she accidentally burned him. As for Rauching's treatment of a runaway slave couple, it appears that he ordered a coffin made for them and then forced them to get into it and buried them alive.

German serfs working in the field for the lord of the manor.
Reproduced by permission of Archive Photos, Inc.

Laws Concerning Slaves and Freedmen

7. And because on the suggestion of many we have found for a certainty that those, who were freed from slavery in the churches according to the custom of the country, have been recalled to slavery again on the whim of all kinds of people, we have deemed it **impious** that those who have been freed from the **yoke** of **servitude** in the Church out of consideration for God should be disregarded. Therefore, because of its piety, it is pleasing to the common council that it be observed, that, whatever slaves be released from servitude by free masters, shall remain in that freedom which they then received from their **lords**. Also liberty of this kind, if it be questioned by any one shall be defended with justice by the churches, except for those faults for which the laws ordered **revocation** of the liberties **conferred on** slaves.

Impious: Ungodly.

Yoke: A type of collar worn by oxen in order to pull loads.

Servitude: The condition of being a servant.

Lords: Owners or masters.

Revocation: Removal.

Conferred on: Given to.

Pledged: Promised, in return for money.

Refuge: Protection.

Unmindful of: Not respecting.

Excommunicated: Forced to give up membership in the Church—a serious punishment in the Middle Ages.

Sanctuary: Refuge, usually taken in a church.

Calumny: False and damaging accusations.

Molestation: Attack.

Gentile: Non-Jewish; in this context, however, it means non-Christian.

Sect: Religious group.

Outside the pale: Beyond the boundaries, or the jurisdiction.

Ecclesiastical: Of the church.

Transgression: Sin or wrongdoing.

Malice: Ill will.

Shins to be bared: To remove clothing from the shin area.

*...14. Concerning freemen who sell themselves for money or other things, or who have **pledged** themselves, it is our pleasure that if they can find the price, as much as was given for them, when the price is given, they shall be restored to their former status without delay, nor shall more be required than was given for them. And meanwhile, if one of them shall have married a free wife, or if one of them, being a woman, shall have taken a freeman as husband, the children who are born of them shall remain free.*

*...22. But concerning slaves, who flee for **refuge** to the church on account of any offense, we decree that it should be observed that they be sent away certain of forgiveness, just as is acknowledged to have been written in ancient laws, after the lord, whoever he may be, has taken the oath to pardon the offense. For, if the lord, **unmindful of** his oath, shall be proved to have broken his promise, and the slave who accepted forgiveness shall be proved to have been punished in some way for that fault, the faithless lord shall be **excommunicated**. Again if the lord has taken the oath and the slave, though safe when pardoned, is unwilling to go and so seeks **sanctuary** because he might perish at the hands of his lord, then his master may seize the unwilling slave so that the Church might suffer no **calumny** nor **molestation** in any way whatsoever as if it had appeared desirous of retaining the slave; nevertheless the lord should by no means break his oath of forgiveness. But if he should be a **gentile** lord or one of another **sect** and be proved to be **outside the pale** of the Church and should seek the return of his slave, he shall have Christians as pledges of good faith who shall take the oaths to the slave on behalf of the lord; because they who fear **ecclesiastical** discipline for their **transgression** are able to keep what is sacred.*

History of the Franks

*[The widow of Godwin] married Rauching, a man of great vanity, swollen with pride, shameless in his arrogance, who acted towards those subject to him as though he were without any spark of human kindness, raging against them beyond the bounds of **malice** and stupidity and doing unspeakable injuries to them. For if, as was customary, a slave held a burning candle before him at dinner, he caused his **shins to be bared**, and placed the candle between them until the*

*flame died; and he caused the same thing to be done with a second candle until the shins of the torchbearer were burned. But if the slave tried to cry out, or to move from one place to another, **a naked sword** threatened him; and he found great enjoyment in the man's tears. They say that at that time two of his slaves, a man and a girl, fell in love—a thing which often happens—and that when their affection for each other had lasted for a period of two years, they fled together to a church. When Rauching found this out he went to the*

A naked sword: That is, a sword removed from its sheath or protective covering.

Christianity and Slavery

The Bible contains ninety references to slaves and slavery, more than half of them in the Old Testament, which is the sacred scripture of the Jewish faith. For example, the Book of Genesis tells the story of how Joseph was sold into slavery in Egypt by his brothers; later, he became one of the most powerful men in the country. In the Book of Genesis, the Egyptian enslavement of the Israelites is described. The latter part of Exodus and several later books contain the records of early Jewish law, including a number of provisions concerning the treatment of slaves.

The birth of Jesus Christ (believed by some to be the savior of the Jews) and the spreading of his teachings, as described in the New Testament, was the beginning of the Christian faith. With his message of God's love for all people, no matter their place in society, Christ might have been expected to condemn slavery; however, his mission was to change people's hearts, not to change laws.

The Apostle Paul, an important figure in the development of Christianity, took Christ's lead. According to Paul's teachings, true slavery was a condition of the spirit rather than the body, since all people are slaves to sin. As for the actual institution of slavery, Paul urged Christian slaves to submit to their masters, not be-

priest of that place and asked him to return the two slaves immediately, saying that he had forgiven them. Then the priest said to him, "You know what **veneration** is due to the churches of God. You cannot take them unless you take an oath to allow them to remain together permanently, and you must also promise that they will be free from **corporal punishment**." But he [Rauching], being in doubt and remaining silent for some time at length turned to the priest and put his hands upon the altar, saying, "They will never be separated by me, but rather I shall cause them to remain in **wedlock**; for though I was annoyed that they did such things without my advice, I am perfectly happy to observe that the man did not take the maid of another in wedlock, nor did she take the slave of another." The **simple** priest believed him and returned the two slaves who had been **ostensibly** pardoned. He [Rauching] took them, gave thanks, and returned to his house, and **straightaway** ordered a tree to be cut down. Then he ordered the trunk to be opened with **wedges** and hollowed out, and a hole to be made in the ground to the depth of three or four feet, and the trunk to be placed therein. Then placing the girl as if she were dead, he ordered the slave to be thrown on top of her. And

Veneration: Respect bordering on worship.

Corporal punishment: Punishment affecting the physical body.

Wedlock: Marriage.

Simple: Not clever; trusting.

Ostensibly: Supposedly.

Straightaway: Immediately.

Wedges: Sharp metal tools.

cause slavery was morally right, but because as Christians they should provide others with an example of peacefulness and gentleness.

These principles are clearly spelled out in the New Testament book of Philemon, actually a letter from Paul to a Christian by that name. Philemon's slave Onesimus had run away, which under the laws of the time was punishable by death; but in the course of his wanderings, Onesimus had met Paul and had converted to Christianity. Paul told Onesimus to return to Philemon, and urged the latter to forgive his slave. Paul offered to pay Philemon for any damage caused by Onesimus.

In the centuries that followed the writing of the New Testament, Christians were divided over the subject of slavery. Those sympathetic to the practice cited the advice of Christ and Paul that slaves should submit to their masters. On the other hand, Christian opponents of slavery noted that both Christ and Paul had taught that all humans are the same in the eyes of God. During the eighteenth and nineteenth centuries, in fact, some of the most outspoken opponents of slavery were Christian leaders such as the preacher John Wesley (1703–1791), whose "Thoughts Upon Slavery" (1774) contained a powerful antislavery message.

when the cover had been placed upon the trunk he filled the grave and buried them both alive, saying, "I have not broken my oath and I have not separated them."

What happened next...

The sixth century in Western Europe was the beginning of a period sometimes described as "the Dark Ages," an era that lasted until about A.D. 1000. For much of this era, Western Europe was in a state of confusion and progress almost came to a standstill. But in the eleventh century, a number of factors propelled Europe out of the Dark Ages.

In 1095, European armies launched a series of wars known as the Crusades, or "wars for the cross," in which they attempted to gain control of the Holy Land (i.e., the Middle East) for the Roman Catholic Church. Although the Crusades ultimately proved to be a failure, they gave Europeans exposure

Gregory of Tours

Gregory of Tours was among the most important historians of the early medieval period in Western Europe. Born Georgius Florentius, he lived most of his life in what is now France, which at that time was ruled by the tribe known as the Franks.

Gregory became the bishop, or the leading Church official, for the city of Tours in 573. For many years, he was involved in a dispute with Chilperic (539–584), a harsh king whose reign was characterized by war, high taxes, and conflict with the clergy, or priests. In addition to *History of the Franks,* Gregory wrote a book on the lives of the saints and one on famous miracles. After his death, he was canonized, or made a saint.

to different parts of the world and hastened the pace of progress in Europe. As a result, Europe's economy grew and people gained more rights, which helped bring about an end of slavery.

Between 1347 and 1351, a widespread disease called the Black Death wiped out nearly a third of Europe's population. As a result, peasants (poor farmers and laborers) were in great demand. Suddenly there were alternatives to serfdom, and many talented peasants made their way to the cities, where they got jobs in skilled professions. Serfdom gradually faded away, and England became the first European country to outlaw it in 1574. The movement to abolish serfdom gradually spread eastward, until it reached Russia in 1861.

Did you know...

- Peasants, or poor farmers, made up about eighty percent of Europe's population during the Middle Ages.

- The term "serf" comes from the Latin word *servus,* meaning "slave."

- The Franks gave their name to the country of France.

For more information

Books

Cave, Roy C. and Herbert H. Coulson, eds. *A Source Book for Medieval Economic History.* Milwaukee, Wis.: Bruce Publishing Co., 1936.

Sources

Books

Compareti, Alice. *Gregory's Angels.* Grand Rapids, Mich.: Eerdmans, 1972.

Macht, Norman L. and Mary Hull. *The History of Slavery.* San Diego, Calif.: Lucent Books, 1997.

Rice, Edward. *A Young People's Pictorial History of the Church.* Adapted by Blanche Jennings Thompson. New York: Farrar, Straus, 1963.

Other

"Medieval Sourcebook: Fifth Council of Orleans: Concerning Freedmen, 549." http://www.fordham.edu/halsall/source/549Orleans.html (accessed on January 12, 2000).

"Medieval Sourcebook: Gregory of Tours: Harsh Treatment of Serfs and Slaves, c. 575." http://www.fordham.edu/halsall/source/575Rauching.html (accessed on January 12, 2000).

James M. Ludlow

"The Tribute of Children"
Published in *The World's Story:*
***A History of the World in Story, Song, and Art*, 1914–18**
Edited by Eva March Tappan

While serfdom (an institution in Europe during the Middle Ages bounding people as servants to lords) became prominent in Europe, traditional slavery remained a significant force in the Middle East. Because of its position between Europe, Africa, and Asia, the region was an important trading center. Local Arab merchants maintained a thriving business in captured Africans and other slaves.

Arab or Middle Eastern slave traders were not concerned with the same issues that eventually brought an end to slavery in America. Whereas many Americans recognized that the practice of slavery was opposed to the principles of freedom and equality spelled out in the U.S. Constitution, slavery did not necessarily go against the principles of the Muslim or Islamic faith, which dominated the Middle East. Like Christianity, Islam made little effort to directly oppose slavery, and many believers in the Islamic faith considered slavery to be justified—particularly if the slaves were members of another religion.

The Turks, a non-Arab people who migrated from Central Asia to modern-day Turkey in the 900s, had a long

They are kept up by continual additions from the sultan's share of the captives, and by recruits, raised every five years, from the children of the Christian subjects.

tradition of slavery; yet unlike Europeans, they did not look down on or think of slaves as inferiors. As a matter of fact, slaves were able to rise to positions of importance in the Turkish government. In the 900s, when Arabs still dominated the Middle East, a number of Turks served in the government as slave-soldiers.

Soon the Turks built a thriving empire that overshadowed the Arab empire. Usually their slave-soldiers came from Muslim families, but in 1388 the Ottoman sultan, or king, Murad created an elite group of slave-soldiers called the Janissaries (JAN-uh-sair-eez), comprised of male children captured from Christian nations.

Things to remember while reading

- The name *Janissaries* (or *Janizaries* as it is used in Ludlow's document) comes from the Turkish *yingi-cheri*, meaning "new soldiers." The following passage makes use of numerous other terms from the Turkish language, some of which are untranslatable.

- By his name, it can be assumed that James M. Ludlow came from an English-speaking country, which in turn means that his upbringing was probably influenced by European and Christian ideas. He maintained the European custom of mistakenly referring to members of the Muslim religion as "Mohammedans." This was a reference to the prophet Muhammad (c. 570–632), founder of the Islamic faith and its holy book the Koran; however, most Muslims considered the term "Mohammedan" offensive, because they worshiped Allah or God and not Muhammad.

- During the era of the Janissaries, Turkey was controlled by the Ottoman Empire, which at different times included a wide array of nations in the Middle East, North Africa, and southeastern Europe. Its base was in present-day Turkey, and a large portion of that region in premodern times was known as Anatolia.

- Among the Ottoman Empire's cities was Adrianopolis, which Ludlow referred to as Adrianople, in northwestern

SPAHIS

IANISSAIRES

A copper engraving of Janissaries, which was an elite group of slave-soldiers made up of male children captured by the Turks from Christian nations.
Reproduced by permission of Corbis-Bettmann.

Turkey. Constantinople was an ancient city, formerly the capital of the Eastern Roman Empire, which is often referred to as the Byzantine Empire. After the Turks defeated the Byzantines in 1453, Constantinople became the Turkish capital, and remained so until the early twentieth century. Today it is known as Istanbul, and Galata is its chief business district. Finally, Saloniki—better known as Salonika—is a city in Greece.

Mohammedan: A European term for Islam, or the Muslim faith.

Consecrated: Committed to God's service.

Dervish: A type of Muslim holy man.

Janizaries (or Janissaries): A group of elite slave-soldiers who directly served the sultan of Ottoman Turkey.

Countenances: Faces, or appearances.

Proverbial: Often mentioned.

Haughty: Proud.

Sultan: A type of king in the Muslim world.

Firman: A type of Turkish official.

Protogeros: A term describing a type of Turkish official.

Seignior: A man of rank or authority.

Tithe: A regular offering, usually consisting of one-tenth of one's income.

Pashas: Men of high rank.

Bohemians: People from what is now the Czech Republic in Central Europe.

Mussulman: A European term for the Muslim religion.

Seraglio: The sultan's palace.

"The Tribute of Children"

...[M]any thousands of the European captives were educated in the **Mohammedan** religion and arms, and the new militia was **consecrated** and named by a celebrated **dervish**. Standing in the front of their ranks, he stretched the sleeve of his gown over the head of the foremost soldier, and his blessing was delivered in the following words "Let them be called **Janizaries**; may their **countenances** be ever bright; their hand victorious; their swords keen; may their spear always hang over the heads of their enemies; and, wheresoever they go, may they return with a white face." White and black face are common and **proverbial** expressions of praise and reproach in the Turkish language. Such was the origin of these **haughty** troops, the terror of the nations.

They are kept up by continual additions from the **sultan's** share of the captives, and by recruits, raised every five years, from the children of the Christian subjects. Small parties of soldiers, each under a leader, and each provided with a particular **firman**, go from place to place. Wherever they come, the **protogeros** assembled the inhabitants with their sons. The leader of the soldiers have the right to take away all the youth who are distinguished by beauty or strength, activity or talent, above the age of seven. He carries them to the court of the grand **seignior**, a **tithe**, as it is, of the subjects. The captives taken in war by the **pashas**, and presented by them to the sultan, include Poles, **Bohemians**, Russians, Italians, and Germans.

These recruits are divided into two classes. Those who compose the one, are sent to Anatolia, where they are trained to agricultural labor, and instructed in the **Mussulman** faith; or they are retained about the **seraglio**, where they carry wood and water, and are employed in the gardens, in the boats, or upon the public buildings, always under the direction of an overseer, who with a stick compels them to work. The others, in whom traces of a higher character are discernible, are placed in one of the four seraglios of Adrianople or Galata, or the old or new one at Constantinople. Here they are lightly clad in linen or in cloth of Saloniki, with caps of **Prusa cloth**. Teachers come every morning, who remain with them until evening, and teach them to read and write. Those who have performed hard labor are made Janizaries. Those who are educated in the seraglios become spahis or higher officers of state.

A slave market in Constantinople, the capital city of the Ottoman Empire. Local Arab slave traders maintained a thriving business in captured Africans and other slaves.
Reproduced by permission of Archive Photos, Inc.

*Both classes are kept under a strict discipline. The former [those training to be Janizaries] especially are accustomed to **privation** of food, drink, and comfortable clothing and to hard labor. They are exercised in shooting with the bow and **arquebuse** by day, and spend the night in a long, lighted hall, with an overseer, who walks up and down, and permits no one to stir. When they are received into the corps of the Janizaries, they are placed in **cloister-like** barracks.... Here not only the younger continue to obey the elders in silence and submission, but all are governed with such strictness that no one is permitted to spend the night abroad, and whoever is punished is compelled to kiss the hand of him who inflicts the punishment.*

*The younger portion, in the seraglios, are kept not less strictly, every ten being committed to the care of an **inexorable** attendant. They are employed in similar exercises, but likewise in study. The grand seignior permitted them to leave the seraglio every three years. Those who choose to remain, **ascend**, according to their age in the immediate service of their master, from **chamber** to chamber, and to constantly greater pay, till they attain, perhaps, to one of the*

Prusa cloth: A type of material highly prized in the Ottoman Empire.

Privation: The act of being deprived of something.

four great posts of the innermost chamber, from which the way to the dignity of a **beglerbeg**, *or a* capitan deiri *(that is, an* **admiral**)*, or even of a* **vizier**, *is open. Those, on the contrary, who take advantage of this permission, enters, each one according to his previous rank, into the four first corps of the paid spahis, who are in the immediate service of the sultan, and in whom he* **confides** *more than in his other bodyguards.*

What happened next...

As Ludlow noted, the Janissaries enjoyed enormous power, and eventually their influence became so great that they had the ability to make or break sultans and other leaders of the Ottoman Empire. The Janissaries continued to exist for more than four hundred years, until 1826 when Sultan Mahmud II (1785–1839) ordered their execution.

By that time, the Ottoman Empire had long since ceased to be a great power. Influence had shifted to European countries, which in the meantime had spawned new forms of slavery by controlling Africans and other peoples. Whereas the institution of the Janissaries had been surrounded with great respect and power, the Europeans, or rather their descendants in other parts of the world, barely regarded their slaves as human beings. Slavery had entered a new, and even more painful, phase.

Did you know...

- The Ottoman Empire, established in approximately 1300, was not formally dissolved until 1922. It existed longer than almost any single political system in history.

- One group of Turkish slave-soldiers, called Mamluks, controlled the government of Egypt for about 250 years.

- The idea of slave-soldiers spread as far east as the Indian subcontinent, parts of which were conquered by Turks. As a matter of fact, a number of former slaves actually became kings in that region.

Arquebuse (or harquebuse): An early type of gun.

Cloister-like: Resembling a cloister or monastery, a place for men who forsake the outside world to pursue quiet, disciplined lives.

Inexorable: Unavoidable.

Ascend: Go up.

Chamber: In this context, it implies a particular position or rank in the government.

Beglerbeg: A type of Turkish officer.

Admiral: A high-ranking naval officer, equivalent to a general in the army.

Vizier: A chief minister.

Confides: Places trust.

The Black Legend

As the Ottoman Empire reached the height of its power, a new phase in the history of slavery was beginning: the European enslavement of Africans and Native Americans in the New World. The first European slavers were the Spanish and Portuguese, who also led Europe in the exploration of Africa and the New World. Almost from the beginning of this practice, however, there were people in these countries that questioned the treatment of non-European peoples. Thus was born the "Black Legend."

This term refers to a type of literature attacking the Spanish system in the Americas. The father of the Black Legend was Bartolomé de Las Casas (1474–1566). Las Casas first came to the New World in 1502 as the owner of a plantation. Ten years after his arrival, he became a priest and began to preach against slavery. He devoted his life to an unsuccessful campaign for the abolition of slavery.

In 1552 Las Casas published the *The Very Brief Account of the Destruction of the Indies* (i.e. the lands inhabited by Indians, or Native Americans). This work helped to spread the "Black Legend" of Spanish cruelty in the New World. Las Casas's writing was heavy-handed; he portrayed all Native Americans as good, and all Spaniards as evil, but no one could doubt his sincerity.

Thanks to the relatively recent invention of printing, his book reached a wide audience. By 1575 it had been translated into French, Dutch, and English. At home in Spain, his writing caused many to question the institution and practice of slavery.

For more information

Books

Tappan, Eva March, ed. *The World's Story: A History of the World in Story, Song, and Art.* 15 volumes. Boston: Houghton Mifflin Company, 1914–18.

Sources

Books

Goodwin, Godfrey. *The Janissaries.* London: Saqi, 1994.

Pallis, Alexander. *In the Days of the Janissaries: Old Turkish Life as Depicted in the 'Travel-Book' of Evilyá Chelebi.* New York: Hutchinson, 1951.

Stewart, Desmond and The Editors of Time-Life Books. *Early Islam.* New York: Time-Life Books, 1967.

Slavery in the Middle East and Africa

Though slavery is most often identified with the descendants of Europeans in the New World (a European term for North and South America), in fact slavery existed in the Middle East from ancient times until recent centuries. Likewise Africans practiced slavery centuries ago, and in the twenty-first century, Africa was one of the few places where traditional slavery (as opposed to newer forms such as child labor) still existed.

People in early Africa did not tend to regard slaves as inferiors, and it was quite likely that a person who was enslaved might later be free, or that a free person might become a slave if he fell into the hands of an enemy tribe. If there was any kind of deep-seated hatred or emotion associated with slavery, it was not racial but tribal; indeed, Africans would later assist European slave traders by selling members of neighboring tribes into slavery.

However, some racial hatred did exist between Arab or Persian (Iranian) slavers and African slaves, whom they referred to as *Zanj*. Middle Eastern writings on the Zanj, which date back to A.D. 680, typically referred to them as a lazy and dishonest people whose dark skin—in the view of the authors—made them inferior to the Arabs and Persians. The writers also believed that the Zanj possessed magical powers.

Yet people in East Africa greatly admired the Arabs, and this made the Africans easy targets for capture. Many of the Zanj became slaves in the Middle East, and in 868 there was a widespread slave revolt. For nearly fifteen years, the rebels controlled much of southern Iraq, but by 883 the Muslim government had suppressed the revolt.

People in the Middle East did not only enslave sub-Saharan or "black" Africans. In fact, people captured in battle—Europeans, East Africans, and many others—often wound up as slaves of Arabs, Persians, or Turks. The Janissaries of the Ottoman Turks, for instance, came from Europe. This was one of the few instances when Europeans or their descendants were the slaves and not the slaveholders.

Other

"Cultural Readings—Viewers and the Viewed—Black Legends." http://www.library.upenn.edu/special/gallery/kislak/viewers/black.html (accessed on January 19, 2000).

"The Enderun and Up-Bringing of Janissaries." http://www.yok.gov.tr/webeng/histedu/part1_3.html (accessed on January 19, 2000).

"Islamic History Sourcebook: James M. Ludlow: The Tribute of Children, 1493." http://www.fordham.edu/halsall/islam/1493Janissaries.html (accessed on January 12, 2000).

"Memoirs of a Janissary." http://www.humanities.ccny.cuny.edu/history/reader/jan.htm (accessed on January 19, 2000).

Early Modern Slavery
(1500–1900)

As the Renaissance (a period of renewed interest in learning) began to sweep Western Europe around 1450, the practice of slavery began to change. A pivotal event was the arrival of fourteen African slaves in Portugal in 1441. The slaves had been captured in the interior by other Africans, who then sold them to a Portuguese mariner on the coast of Africa. The mariner in turn brought them back to Europe, where he presented the slaves to Prince Henry the Navigator (1394–1460).

Although he never really traveled, Prince Henry was the guiding force in an age of Portuguese exploration. Under his direction, Portuguese sailors charted the coast of Africa and sea routes to India. Portuguese economic interest in Africa was motivated primarily by goods such as gold and ivory; slaves were, at least at first, an afterthought. After all, slavery was not practiced in Europe, since there was no shortage of cheap labor.

However, the discovery of the New World (a European term for North and South America) by Christopher Columbus in 1492 left the Spanish with vast new territories with a seemingly limitless need for labor. At first the Spanish conquerors attempted to enslave the peoples they called "Indians," the native inhabitants of the New World. This proved futile for a number of reasons, one being the fact that the Native Americans, lacking previous exposure to European diseases such as smallpox, died by the thousands.

Therefore, European interest turned to the African slave trade. In 1518, the first slaves from West Africa arrived in the New World, where they worked on plantations in the West Indies. In 1619, the first African slaves arrived at the English colony in Jamestown, Virginia. In the years that followed, three areas of the New World became centers of large slave populations: Cuba and the West Indies (that is, the islands of the Caribbean); Brazil; and the southern United States.

Partly as a result of their British cultural heritage, with its relatively high respect for human rights, Americans placed a great value on freedom; this made the existence of slavery in the United States all the more ironic. The writing of **Alexander Falconbridge**, a British doctor who served aboard a slave ship, amply illustrates his country's humanitarian tradition. However, the recollections of **James Barbot**, also an Englishman, but a slave trader confident that there was nothing morally wrong with slavery, make it clear that this humanitarian tradition had its limits.

Underlying Barbot's account was a belief that Africans were less than human, which made it possible for Europeans to engage in the slave trade without suffering a crisis of conscience. Perhaps it was true that humans had certain rights that could not be taken from them, as the U.S. Declaration of Independence stated in 1776; but if a person was not really a complete human being, then those rights could be disregarded. This was the essence of racism, one of the factors that set early modern slavery apart from the slavery in earlier eras. In order for slavery to exist along the values of freedom and justice adopted not only by the British but also increasingly by other Europeans, it was necessary to treat certain races as inferior to others.

By the early 1800s, Britain had outlawed the slave trade, and most European countries were on their way to enacting provisions that would make slavery illegal. The United States had passed feeble laws against slave trading, but these were not well enforced, and they only increased the demand

in some quarters that slavery be abolished entirely. This was the position of the **American Antislavery Society** (AAS), a leading organization in the abolitionist movement. Its 1833 "Declaration of Sentiments" made it clear that the abolitionists viewed persons of African descent as the equals of all other Americans—and that therefore slavery should be abolished as an offense to human dignity.

Such statements were powerful weapons against slavery. Another effective tool was the publication of slave narratives, which were autobiographical books or articles by people raised under slavery. They offered compelling evidence of the human suffering inflicted by the practice of slavery. An example was the article by a slave whose name appears to have been Ralph, but who was listed simply as "**Anonymous**" when his autobiography appeared in *Putnam's Monthly Magazine* in 1857.

By that point, America was well on its way to the Civil War (1861–65), a conflict that would decide the slavery

The arrival of the first African slaves at Jamestown, Virginia, in 1619.
Courtesy of The Library of Congress.

African slave traders leading a group of captured Africans to the coast to be sold as slaves. Without the help of African slave traders, Europeans could have never penetrated the interior of the African continent and kidnaped slaves.
Reproduced by permission of The Granger Collection.

harsh as the treatment of African slaves by Europeans. It is also important to note that the Europeans could never have penetrated the interior of the African continent and kidnaped slaves on their own: they needed the help of African slave traders who lived on the Atlantic coast and were willing to sell out members of other tribes.

The Portuguese were slave traders, and both Spaniards and Portuguese in the New World—where Portugal's colony of Brazil became a vast slave empire—used slave labor. By the 1700s, however, both Spain and Portugal were eclipsed by new powers: Britain and France. In some ways, the two new powers resembled the old ones. For example, Spain, like France, was not actively involved in the actual slave trade, but it certainly made use of slaves in its New World colonies. Like Portugal before it, Britain took an active role both in the slave trade and in the slave system as it existed in the New World.

To a much greater extent than Spain, Portugal, or even France, Britain had a strong and growing tradition of respect for individual freedom and human dignity. Given such views it was difficult to justify the buying and selling of human beings. Many concerned people became abolitionists, or opponents of slavery, and one of their leading figures was Alexander Falconbridge, a surgeon who had worked aboard slave ships during the mid1700s.

Things to remember while reading

- The following passage, condensed from Falconbridge's *An Account of the Slave Trade on the Coast of Africa* (1788), describes aspects of slavery, beginning with the point at which slaves were sold by slavers at markets in West Africa. At these markets, the sellers were Africans, and the buyers Europeans. The slaves were forced onto prison-like ships, where they sailed to the New World amid horrible conditions.

- With his unique perspective, Falconbridge paid special attention to the health hazards posed to the slaves by the close, confined quarters in which they were kept. At one point when he was tending to patients in the slave hold, he noted, it became so unbearably hot that he could only stay down there for a few minutes at a time. As a free man, Falconbridge had the option of going above decks; the captives did not.

Alexander Falconbridge

Alexander Falconbridge was a British surgeon who worked aboard slave ships during the mid to late 1700s. Disgusted by the treatment of captured Africans, Falconbridge resolved to expose the slave traders inhumane behavior. The result was *An Account of the Slave Trade on the Coast of Africa* (1788).

Falconbridge's book began with the words, "The following sheets [pages] are intended to lay before the public the present state of a branch of the British commerce [economy], which, ever since its existence, has been held in detestation [hatred] by all good men, but at this time more particularly engages the attention of the nation, and is become the object of general reprobation [disapproval]." The book described almost the entire process of slave trading: the purchase of slaves from slavers (who, like the slaves, were Africans) along the African coast; the harsh treatment of the captives on the voyage to the Americas; and finally, the sale of slaves in the islands of the West Indies.

Falconbridge was popular with English abolitionists. He became governor of Sierra Leone, a newly created colony for freed slaves, but he was later removed from office. He died in 1792.

- Falconbridge may have been unaware of the deeper meaning of his words when, in several places, he noted that circumstances aboard the ship often caused the slaves to quarrel with one another. No doubt the slave traders *wanted* the slaves to fight amongst themselves, so that they would not join forces against their common enemy. Also, his description of how the slaves were forced to sing and dance is intriguing. Even in modern times, African Americans are sometimes stereotyped, or lumped together in a misleading and racist way, as accomplished singers and dancers; the passage from Falconbridge shows how many slaves developed these abilities as a survival technique.

- From what Falconbridge wrote in the third paragraph from the last, it appears that though the sailors were raping the African women, they had managed to convince themselves that the women engaged in sex willingly. Thus if a woman was raped by one man and then another, it seemed that she was being "unfaithful" to the first man. Even Falconbridge seems to have been misled to an extent, because he referred to the sailors "procuring the consent" of African women. It is hard to imagine a situation in which any of the latter would willingly have engaged in relationships with their captors.

An Account of the Slave Trade on the Coast of Africa

*From forty to two hundred Negroes are generally purchased at a time by the **black traders**, according to the **opulence** of the buyer, and consist of all ages, from a month to sixty years and upwards. Scarcely any age or situation is **deemed** an exception, the price being **proportionable**. Women sometimes form a part of them, who happen to be so far advanced in their pregnancy as to be delivered during their journey from the [slave trading] fairs to the coast; and I have frequently seen instances of deliveries on board ship....*

*[T]he European purchasers ... first examine them [the slaves] **relative to** their age. They then **minutely** inspect their persons and*

Black traders: Slave traders.

Opulence: Wealth.

Deemed: Judged.

Proportionable: Proportionate, or of appropriate size (for the age of the slave.)

Relative to...: In other words, "with regard to..."; or "in terms of...."

Minutely: In detail.

inquire into the state of their health; if they are inflicted with any disease or are deformed or have bad eyes or teeth; if they are lame or weak in the joints or distorted in the back or of *a slender make* or narrow in the chest; in short, if they have been ill or are afflicted in any manner so as to render them incapable of much labor....

The men Negroes, on being brought aboard the ship, are immediately fastened together, two and two, by handcuffs on their wrists and by irons *riveted* on their legs....

[T]hey are frequently *stowed* so close, as to *admit of* no other position than lying on their sides. Nor will the height between decks, unless directly under the *grating*, permit the *indulgence* of an erect posture; especially where there are *platforms*, which is generally the case....

In each of the *apartments* are placed three or four large buckets, of a *conical* form, nearly two feet in diameter at the bottom and only one foot at the top and in depth of about twenty-eight inches, to which, when necessary, the Negroes have *recourse*. It often happens that those who are placed at a distance from the buckets, in *endeavoring* to get to them, tumble over their companions, in consequence of their being *shackled*. These accidents, although unavoidable, *are productive of* continual quarrels in which some of them are always bruised. In this distressed situation, unable to proceed and prevented from getting to the tubs, they *desist from the attempt*; and as *the necessities of nature* are not to be resisted, ease themselves as they lie. This becomes a fresh source of *boils and disturbances* and tends to render the condition of the poor captive *wretches* still more uncomfortable....

Their food is served up to them in tubs about the size of a small water bucket. They are placed round these tubs, in companies of ten to each tub, out of which they feed themselves with wooden spoons. These they soon lose and when they are not allowed others they feed themselves with their hands....

Upon the Negroes refusing to take *sustenance*, I have seen coals of fire, glowing hot, put on a shovel and placed so near their lips as to scorch and burn them. And this has been accompanied with threats of forcing them to swallow the coals if they any longer persisted in refusing to eat. These means have generally had the desired effect. I have also been *credibly* informed that a certain captain in the slave-trade, poured melted lead on such of his Negroes as *obstinately* refused their food.

A slender make: A thin body.

Riveted: Fastened with iron pins.

Stowed: To place.

Admit of: Allow.

Grating: An air vent covered with an iron grate.

Indulgence: Freedom or relaxation.

Platforms: In order to put more slaves on board, slave ships usually had a halfdeck midway between the upper and lower deck of the cargo hold.

Apartments: Compartments (in the cargo hold).

Conical: Coneshaped.

Recourse: Access.

Endeavoring: Trying.

Shackled: Chained.

Are productive of: Produce, or cause.

Desist from the attempt: Give up.

The necessities of nature: In this case, the need to go to the bathroom.

Boils and disturbances: Sores and illnesses.

Wretches: Unfortunate people.

Sustenance: Food and/or water.

Credibly: Reliably.

Obstinately: Stubbornly.

*Exercise being deemed necessary for the preservation of their health they are sometimes **obliged** to dance when the weather will permit their coming on deck. If they go about it reluctantly or do not move with **agility**, they are **flogged***

*.... The poor wretches are frequently compelled to sing also; but when they do so, their songs are generally, as may naturally be expected, **melancholy lamentations** of their exile from their native country.*

*The women are furnished with beads for the purpose of affording them some **diversion**. But this end is generally defeated by the squabbles which **are occasioned in consequence of** their stealing from each other.*

*On board some ships the common sailors are allowed to have intercourse with such of the black women whose consent they can **procure**. And some of them have been known to take the **inconstancy** of their **paramours** so much to heart as to leap overboard and drown themselves. The officers are permitted to indulge their passions among them at pleasure and sometimes are guilty of such excesses as disgrace human nature....*

*The hardships and inconveniences suffered by the Negroes during the passage are scarcely to be **enumerated or conceived**....*

*During the voyages I made, I was frequently witness to the fatal effects of this exclusion of fresh air [from the cargo hold]. I will give one instance, as it serves to convey some idea, though a very faint one, of their terrible sufferings.... Some wet and blowing weather having occasioned the port-holes to be shut and the grating to be covered, **fluxes** and fevers among the Negroes **ensued**. While they were in this situation, I frequently went down among them till at length their room became so extremely hot as to be only bearable for a very short time. But the excessive heat was not the only thing that rendered their situation intolerable. The deck, that is the floor of their rooms, was so covered with the blood and mucus which had proceeded from them in consequence of the flux, that it resembled a slaughter-house. It is not in the power of the human imagination to picture a situation more dreadful or disgusting. Numbers of the slaves having fainted, they were carried upon deck where several of them died and the rest with great difficulty were restored....*

Obliged: Forced.

Agility: Grace and speed.

Flogged: Whipped.

Melancholy: Sad.

Lamentations: To lament is to mourn or cry over something.

Diversion: Entertainment.

Are occasioned in consequence of...: I.e., "are a result of...."

Procure: Obtain.

Inconstancy: Unfaithfulness.

Paramours: Lovers.

Enumerated or conceived: In other words, "listed or imagined."

Fluxes: A general term describing discharge of bodily fluids, though most likely the particular condition described was diarrhea.

Ensued: happened as a result.

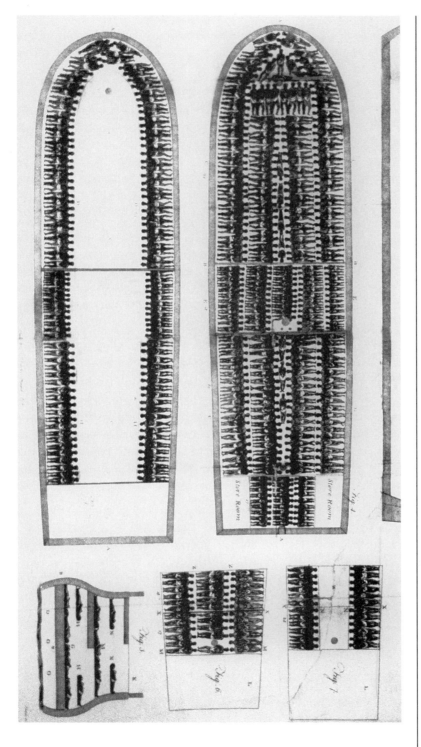

A diagram of a British slave ship showing the layout for stowing 292 slaves. In order to put more slaves on a ship, many slaves were forced to lay in extremely cramped quarters for the entire trip.
Courtesy of The Library of Congress.

Early Slave Narratives

One type of valuable firsthand source about African slavery comes from writers such as Alexander Falconbridge—that is, those rare Europeans who were concerned with the cruelty and injustice of the slave trade. An even more direct account of the slave trade, however, comes from those who experienced it from the worst possible perspective: as slaves.

Among such people was the author of *A Narrative of the Most Remarkable Particulars in the Life of James Albert Ukawsaw Gronniosaw, an African Prince, Written by Himself* (1774). Gronniosaw had begun his life as a member of a powerful African family; later, he had been captured and sold into slavery, but had eventually been able to obtain his freedom. Except for the part about having been a prince, Gronniosaw's story was much the same as that of other former slaves who wrote their life stories in the eighteenth century.

Perhaps the most famous of the slave narrative authors was Olaudah Equiano (c. 1750–1797), also known as Gustavus Vassa. A member of the Ibo people in

What happened next...

Falconbridge's account was actually written a few years after James Barbot (see entry) described a shipboard revolt, but such revolts became more common. Certainly it is easy to understand how and why slaves would want to rise up against their oppressors, given the dreadful conditions to which they were subjected.

By the time of Falconbridge, slavery in the New World was in full swing. Two countries took the lead in the slave trade: Britain, with its slave trading ships and colonies; and the brand-new American republic, with its southern regions heavily dependent on agricultural slave labor. Yet these were also the lands that claimed to value liberty and individual rights the most.

Did you know...

- Slaves did not come from all over Africa; rather, they were taken almost entirely from the western part of the

what is now Nigeria, Equiano was kidnaped at age eleven and sold into slavery. He was sent first to Barbados, one of the main slaveholding islands of the West Indies, but eventually wound up in Virginia. There he served a British naval officer, who then sold him to a Quaker merchant from Philadelphia, Pennsylvania. The Quakers, a religious group, had strong antislavery sentiments, and in 1766 the merchant allowed Equiano to purchase his freedom.

Equiano spent the remainder of his life as an active participant in the abolitionist, or antislavery, movement. In 1789, he published *The Interesting Narrative of the Life of Olaudah Equiano or Gustavus Vassa the African.* The book included a description of his capture. One day while his parents were out tending their crops, Equiano wrote, two men and a woman—apparently Africans—kidnaped him and his sister: "without giving us time to cry out, or make resistance, they stopped our mouths, and ran off with us into the nearest wood."

continent—the enormous "hump" of Africa that extends into the Atlantic Ocean.

- Ironically, West Africa had been the site of numerous great and wealthy civilizations, such as Ghana, Mali, and the Songhai Empire, just a few centuries before the slave ships arrived.

- One British philosopher whose ideas inspired the antislavery movement was John Locke (1632–1704). Locke wrote that all human beings deserved certain natural rights, which he identified as "life, liberty, and the pursuit of property." This inspired the reference to "life, liberty, and the pursuit of happiness" in the U.S. Declaration of Independence.

For more information

Books

Falconbridge, Alexander. *An Account of the Slave Trade on the Coast of Africa.* London: J. Phillips, 1788.

Sources

Books

Frank, Andrew. *The Birth of Black America: The Age of Discovery and the Slave Trade.* New York: Chelsea House, 1996.

OfosuAppiah, L. H. *People in Bondage: African Slavery Since the 15th Century.* Minneapolis, Minn.: Runestone Press, 1993.

White, Anne Terry. *Human Cargo: The Story of the Atlantic Slave Trade.* Champaign, Ill.: Garrard Publishing Company, 1972.

Other

"Alexander Falconbridge's Account of the Slave Trade." http:/www.pbs. org/wgbh/aia/part1/1h281.html (accessed on January 20, 2000).

"The American Nation—Alexander Falconbridge, The African Slave Trade (1788)." http://longman.awl.com/garraty/primarysource_2_ 13.htm (accessed on January 20, 2000).

"The Impact of Slavery." *African History Sourcebook.* http://www.fordham. edu/halsall/africa/africasbook.html#The Impact of Slavery (accessed on January 20, 2000).

"The Middle Passage." *Juneteenth.* http://www.juneteenth.com/middlep. htm (accessed on January 20, 2000).

James Barbot

Excerpt from "A Supplement to the Description of the Coasts of North and South Guinea"
Published in *A Collection of Voyages and Travels...*, 1732
Compiled by Awnsham Churchill

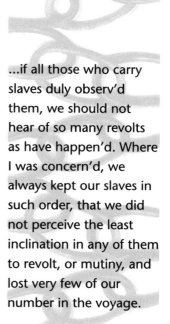

O ne of the most frequently used terms in the vocabulary of slavery is "Middle Passage." This is a reference to the triangular route employed by most slave ships, the middle part of which was the voyage from Africa to the New World. Ships would sail from Europe to West Africa, where they would pick up slaves; then from Africa to the Americas, where they would sell the slaves for goods such as corn and tobacco; and then from the New World back to Europe, where they sold the products.

If one forgets for a moment that slavers were trafficking in human lives, and instead views this arrangement in pure business terms, it makes sense: rather than send empty ships on a transatlantic voyage, European merchants were able to make money on both the journey out and the journey back. The fact is that although slavery was an extraordinarily cruel business, it was a business nonetheless, and the people who engaged in it considered it as just another way to make a living. This was the perspective of James Barbot, a crew member aboard the English slave ship *Don Carlos*.

In the following passage, Barbot describes the same situations observed by Alexander Falconbridge (see entry),

...if all those who carry slaves duly observ'd them, we should not hear of so many revolts as have happen'd. Where I was concern'd, we always kept our slaves in such order, that we did not perceive the least inclination in any of them to revolt, or mutiny, and lost very few of our number in the voyage.

Slave Rebellions

In 1838 the only successful slave ship rebellion in United States history occurred aboard the *Amistad,* a Spanish ship from Cuba. Soon after the slaves revolted, they chose as their leader Joseph Cinque (c. 1810–c. 1880). Their ship wound up in the United States, where the slaves went on trial, and eventually the case went before the U.S. Supreme Court. Defended by former U.S. President John Quincy Adams (1767–1848; President 1825–1829), the slaves won the case in 1841, and Cinque and the other mutineers were freed.

On at least one occasion, slaves in the New World established their own governments. This happened in northeastern Brazil, where the Republic of Palmares—founded and governed by escaped slaves—existed between 1630 and 1697. Palmares, destroyed by the Portuguese in 1697, represented by far the longest running slave revolt in the New World.

More tragic was the rebellion led by Toussaint L'Ouverture (1743–1803) in Haiti, which was a French colony with a huge slave population. The revolt began in

but with a very different attitude. Barbot's description begins with an account of a slave revolt, which the slavers brutally suppressed.

Sadly, Barbot was probably correct when he indicated that he and his shipmates treated slaves better than most other crews. Some slavers, as Barbot noted, took out their anger and frustration on the defenseless slaves. In Barbot's mind, however, this was unwise since hurting slaves was not good business.

Things to remember while reading

- As a crew member and not an officer, Barbot was not a particularly well-educated man, and in places his writing is awkward and labored. His unusual spellings, however, are more a product of his era than of his education. At that time, it was common, for instance, to write *crouds* instead of *crowds.* Another regular practice was the use of apostrophes: *arm'd* instead of *armed,* for example.

1791, and led to the abolition of slavery in all French colonies three years later. Yet after Napoleon (1769–1821) became dictator of France in 1799, he was determined to win new territories and gain back ones that had been lost, including Haiti. His troops captured Toussaint, who died in a French prison in 1803. The war in Haiti had exhausted the French, however, and they granted the country its independence early in 1805.

In the United States, there were approximately two hundred slave revolts, most notable being the ones led by Denmark Vesey (1767–1822) in 1822 and Nat Turner (1800–1831) in 1831. Both men were executed for their part in the uprisings. The last major slave related revolt in the United States was an 1859 attack on an ammunition storehouse at Harper's Ferry, Virginia. Leading the raid was John Brown (1800–1859), a white man who hoped to incite a widespread slave revolt. Instead he was captured and executed, and the incident helped bring about the Civil War (1861–65), which resulted in the end of slavery.

- Barbot clearly looked down on the Africans as "savage people" who, like children, would behave themselves if treated properly. At one point, he referred to them as smelling poorly, but it does not seem to have occurred to him that anyone would smell bad if forced to travel under such harsh conditions.

- Throughout his recollections, Barbot congratulated his shipmates for their kind treatment of the slaves. In a section removed from the following passage, he noted that they tried to allow the slaves as much headroom as possible in the cargo hold: "the greater height it has, the more airy and convenient it is for a considerable number of human creatures; and consequently far the more healthy for them, and fitter to look after them."

- On the other hand, Barbot seemed entirely ignorant regarding the cruelty of slavery. Particularly disturbing is his reference to the "abundance of recreation" he and other slavers had with female slaves. The implication here is that they raped the more attractive girls.

Indiscreetly: Unwisely.

Forecastle: The crew's quarters, usually in the bow, or front part of a ship.

Fell: Attacked.

Parcels: Small groups.

Stoutest: Strongest.

Expir'd (i.e., expired): Died.

Boatswain: An officer in charge of maintaining the hull, or the body of the ship, along with other duties.

Pipe: Windpipe.

Terrif'd: Terrified.

Dispersing: Spreading.

Mutinous: Defiant.

Resolution: Determination.

Shewing: Showing.

Betwixt: Between—in this case, between decks, to the narrow cargo hold where slaves were kept.

Good words: In this context, "good words" probably refers to warnings regarding what would happen to slaves who revolted again.

Contrivers: Planners.

Mutiny: Uprising.

Office: Job.

Mortality: Death rate.

Want: Lack.

Us'd: Used.

Prudent: Wise.

"A Supplement to the Description of the Coasts of North and South Guinea"

*About one in the afternoon, after dinner, we, according to custom caused them [the slaves], one by one, to go down between decks, to have each his pint of water; most of them were yet above deck, many of them provided with knives, which we had **indiscreetly** given them two or three days before, as [we were] not suspecting the least attempt of this nature from them; others had pieces of iron they had torn off our **forecastle** door.... Thus arm'd, they **fell** in crouds and **parcels** on our men ... and stabb'd one of the **stoutest** of us all, who receiv'd fourteen or fifteen wounds of their knives, and so **expir'd**. Next they assaulted our **boatswain**, and cut one of his legs so round the bone, that he could not move, the nerves being cut through; others cut our cook's throat to the **pipe**, and others wounded three of the sailors, and threw one of them overboard in that condition, from the forecastle into the sea.... [W]e stood in arms, firing on the revolted slaves, of whom we kill'd some, and wounded many: which so **terrif'd** the rest, that they gave way, **dispersing** themselves .... and many of the most **mutinous**, leapt over board, and drown'd themselves in the ocean with much **resolution**, **shewing** no manner of concern for life. Thus we lost twenty seven or twenty eight slaves, either kill'd by us, or drown'd; and having master'd them, caused all to go **betwixt** decks, giving them **good words**. The next day we had them all again upon deck, where they unanimously declar'd, the Menbombe slaves had been the **contrivers** of the **mutiny**, and for an example we caused about thirty of the ringleaders to be very severely whipt by all our men that were capable of doing that **office**....*

*I have observ'd, that the great **mortality**, which so often happens in slave ships, proceeds as well from taking in too many, as from **want** of knowing how to manage them aboard....*

*It is true, we allow'd them much more liberty, and **us'd** them with more tenderness than most other Europeans would think **prudent** to do; [such] as, to have them all upon deck every day in good weather; to take their meals twice a-day, at fix'd hours, that is, at ten in the morning, and at five at night; which being ended, we made the men go down again between the decks; for the women*

*were almost entirely **at their own discretion**, to be upon deck as long as they pleas'd, **nay** even many of the males had the same liberty **by turns, successively**; few or none being **fetter'd** or kept in shackles, and that only on account of some disturbances, or injuries, **offer'd to** their fellow captives, as will unavoidably happen among a numerous croud of such savage people. Besides, we allow'd each of them ... now and then short pipes and tobacco to smoak upon deck by turns, and some coconuts; and to the women a piece of coarse cloth to cover them, and the same to many of the men, which we took care they did wash from time to time, to prevent **vermin**, which they are very subject to; and because it look'd sweeter and more agreeable. Toward the evening they **diverted** themselves on the deck, as they thought fit, some conversing together, others dancing, singing, and **sporting** after their manner, which pleased them highly, and often **made us pastime**; especially the female sex, who being apart from the males, on the quarterdeck, and many of them young **sprightly** maidens, full of **jollity** and good-humour, afforded us abundance of recreation; as did several little fine boys, which we mostly kept to attend on us about the ship....*

A group of male slaves clubbing a white sailor during a slave revolt like the one described by James Barbot.
Etching from Harper's Weekly. *Courtesy of The Library of Congress.*

At their own discretion: Free.

Nay: No; in this context it means "in fact."

By turns, successively: Not all at the same time.

Fetter'd (or fettered): Chained.

Offer'd to...: I.e., "caused against...."

*Much more might be said relating to the preservation and maintenance of slaves in such voyages, which I leave to the prudence of the officers that govern aboard ... and shall only add these few **particulars**, that tho' we ought to be **circumspect** in watching the slaves narrowly, to prevent or disappoint their ill designs for our own conservation, yet must we not be too severe and **haughty** with them, but on the contrary, caress and **humor them in every reasonable thing**. Some commanders ... are perpetually beating and **curbing** them, even without the least offence, and will not **suffer** any upon deck ... under pretence it hinders the work of the ship and sailors and that they are troublesome by their nasty nauseous stench, or their noise; which makes those poor wretches desperate, and besides their falling into **distempers** thro' melancholy, often is the occasion of their destroying themselves.*

*Such officers should consider, those unfortunate creatures are men as well as themselves, tho' of a different colour, and **pagans**; and that they ought to do to others as they would **be done by** in like circumstances....*

Vermin: Pests; in this case probably lice.

Diverted: Entertained.

Sporting: Playing.

Made us pastime: In other words, "provided us with entertainment."

Sprightly: Healthy.

Jollity: The quality of being jolly.

Particulars: Specifics.

Circumspect: Careful.

Haughty: Fierce.

Humor them in every reasonable thing: I.e., let them have their way whenever possible.

Curbing: Restricting.

Suffer: Allow.

Distempers: Illnesses.

Pagans: People who worship many gods instead of just one.

Be done by: I.e., want to be treated.

What happened next...

It is hard to know what to think of Barbot's final paragraph, with its reference to Christianity's Golden Rule. ("Do unto others as you would have them do unto you.") Perhaps this is evidence that Barbot felt a degree of compassion for the slaves. Or perhaps he was merely being a hypocrite—someone who pretends they are doing the right thing when they know they are not.

On the other hand, Barbot may have believed in the popular justification of slavery on religious grounds. Some religions taught that by enslaving Africans (who were considered heathens), Europeans and their descendants in the Americas were providing them with an opportunity to save themselves from hell by becoming Christians. In this way, many slave traders and owners justified their participation in the practice of slavery.

Certainly supporters of slavery could find passages in the Bible to justify the institution, but many other Christians maintained that slavery went against Christian principles. Together with non-Christians who likewise opposed slavery on moral grounds (i.e., as an offense to the basic dignity of humankind) they began putting pressure on the American and British governments to end the slave trade.

An engraving showing the hold of the slave ship *Gloria*. During their trip to the New World slaves were often force to remain in cramped quarters with little food or water.
Reproduced by permission of The Granger Collection.

Did you know...

- The European trade in African slaves began in 1441, when fourteen slaves were brought to Lisbon, Portugal, as a "gift" to Prince Henry the Navigator (1394–1460).

- The first slaves to cross the Atlantic Ocean on European ships were not Africans bound for the New World, but Native Americans taken *from* the New World to Europe. In 1495, Christopher Columbus returned to Spain with

Indentured Servants

Many people came to the New World in a situation only slightly better than slavery: indentured servitude. In return for passage to the New World, and for room and board while there (as well as, in some cases, clothing or even land), indentured servants agreed to work for a set period of time. Unlike slaves, who were African, indentured servants included not only Africans, but also poor whites from Europe, and Indians from India.

Also unlike slaves, indentured servants had a contract, or a legal document, which outlined the terms of their service—including its duration, which was typically between two and fourteen years. Obviously, the fact that they knew when their service would end made indentured servitude preferable to slavery; however, the conditions of travel to the New World were not much better for indentured servants than for slaves. In addition, indentured servants were often treated like slaves, with long hours, substandard living conditions, and beatings.

several hundred Indian slaves. Most of these men and women died soon after their arrival in Spain.

- Between 1451 and 1870, some eleven million African slaves were brought to the Americas.

For more information

Books

Churchill, Awnsham, compiler. *A Collection of Voyages and Travels, Some Now First Printed from Original Manuscripts, Others Now First Published in English.... With a General Preface, Giving an Account of the Progress of Navigation, from its First Beginning.* London: J. Walthoe, 1732.

Sources

Books

Frank, Andrew. *The Birth of Black America: The Age of Discovery and the Slave Trade.* New York: Chelsea House, 1996.

OfosuAppiah, L. H. *People in Bondage: African Slavery Since the 15th Century.* Minneapolis, Minn.: Runestone Press, 1993.

White, Anne Terry. *Human Cargo: The Story of the Atlantic Slave Trade.* Champaign, Ill.: Garrard Publishing Company, 1972.

Other

Africans in America. http:/www.pbs.org/wgbh/aia/ (accessed on January 20, 2000).

"The Impact of Slavery." *African History Sourcebook.* http://www.fordham.edu/halsall/africa/africasbook.html#The Impact of Slavery (accessed on January 20, 2000).

"The Middle Passage." *Juneteenth.* http://www.juneteenth.com/middlep.htm (accessed on January 20, 2000).

American Antislavery Society

Excerpt from "Declaration of Sentiments"
Published in *The Abolitionists: A Collection of Their Writing*, 1963
Edited by Louis Ruchames

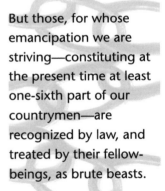

With the signing of the Declaration of Independence in 1776 and the adoption of the U.S. Constitution in 1787, a new government based on what Americans believed were the natural rights of human beings was created. Those rights had a number of dimensions, but they all reduced to a single idea: freedom. And yet when Americans looked around them, they saw that many people were not free.

During the first half of the nineteenth century, the United States became increasingly divided over the question of slavery. To wealthy Southern plantation owners, slavery was believed to be necessary for their economic survival. The invention of the cotton gin, a machine for separating cotton fibers from seeds, had made cotton highly profitable. Along with tobacco, rice, and other crops grown by slaves, it became a mainstay of the economy of the American South.

In the North, however, it was too cold to build an economic system based on agriculture; this turned out to be a blessing in disguise. The North focused on manufacturing goods, such as turning Southern cotton into clothing. These factories competed with those in England, which then led the

But those, for whose emancipation we are striving—constituting at the present time at least one-sixth part of our countrymen—are recognized by law, and treated by their fellow-beings, as brute beasts.

industrialized world. As a result, the material wealth of the North grew much faster than that of the South.

Because the North did not rely on slaves for its economic growth, it was there that the first voices of opposition to slavery made themselves known. In fact, most Northern states had outlawed slavery by the early part of the nineteenth century, and in 1807 the United States prohibited the importation of slaves from overseas. Britain did the same thing a year later, but whereas the British laws proved effective, the American ones did not: too many people, including ship owners from the North, profited from the slave trade.

One possible solution to the slavery problem was the creation of a country in Africa to which freed slaves could return. Thus in 1816 the American Colonization Society formed with a plan to ship former slaves to the nation that would later become Liberia. A few years later, the Missouri Compromise (1820–21) offered another, highly complicated, solution. It admitted two new states to the Union: Missouri, in which slavery was legal, and Maine, in which it was not; and it outlawed slavery in all other states north of Missouri's southern boundary.

Even with these compromises, the debate over slavery continued to escalate, and there was a rising tide of sentiment among many whites in the North (along with a few freed slaves) for the complete abolition, or outlawing, of slavery throughout the United States. Thus was born the abolitionist movement, which consisted of a number or organizations. Most prominent among these was the American Antislavery Society (AAS), formed in 1833 under the leadership of William Lloyd Garrison (1805–1879) and others.

Things to remember while reading

- Abolitionists saw themselves both as Christians and as Americans. Slavery, as they made clear in the Declaration of Sentiments of the American Antislavery Society (AAS), went against both the principles of Christianity and those of the American political system. For instance, the Declaration of Sentiments mentions "Ex. xxi, 16"—that is, the sixteenth verse of the twenty-first chapter of the Old Testament Book of Exodus. Accord-

ing to this passage, found in the King James version of the Bible, "... he that stealeth [i.e., kidnaps] a man, and selleth him ... he shall surely be put to death." Thus throughout the Declaration of Sentiments, the abolitionists referred to slavery as a sin. They also note that America's Founding Fathers had demanded freedom, and that without an end to slavery, America's quest for freedom would be incomplete.

- In line with their beliefs as Christians and Americans, abolitionists regarded it as a self-evident fact—something as obvious as the heat of the Sun or the blue color of the sky, for instance—that slavery was evil. In their view, any laws that legalized slavery were illegal because they went against natural law. The idea that human beings had natural rights had inspired the American Revolution (1775–83), as well as the French Revolution of 1789. Tied in with this concept was that of a social contract, or "social compact" as abolitionists called it. The

Slaves picking cotton on a Southern plantation. Since crops such as cotton became the mainstay of the Southern economy during the mid-1800s, Southern plantation owners believed that slavery was necessary for their economic survival. *Courtesy of The Library of Congress.*

The executive committee of the American Antislavery Society (AAS). Like other abolitionist groups, the AAS believed that a strong nonviolent movement was needed to change the laws regarding slavery.

Reproduced by permission of the Friends Historical Library of Swarthmore College.

social contract refers to the mutual obligations that hold a society together. According to the social contract, people protect their own rights by protecting those of their neighbors.

- There are many references to law throughout the Declaration of Sentiments—for instance, the laws in most Southern states which made it a crime to teach a slave how to read and write, thus keeping them in "heathenish darkness." The abolitionists also note—without naming—the 1807 law outlawing the slave trade. Thus, they reasoned that the institution of American slavery must surely be as serious as the African slave trade.

- This view of slaves as Americans was a progressive one at that time. Tied in with this was the abolitionists' belief that a black person ought to enjoy the same rights as a white person—again, a highly unusual sentiment for any white American in 1833.

- The abolitionists opposed the move to resettle freed blacks in Africa because they believed it was not comparable to allowing the slaves the rights and freedom they deserved as Americans. The abolitionists demanded the immediate freeing of slaves, and did not believe that Southern slave owners should be paid for giving up property that did not belong to them in the first place. However, abolitionists made it clear that they respected the rights of each state to make its own decision regarding slavery, and rejected any attempt by the federal government to settle the question by force. What was needed, the abolitionists held, was a strong nonviolent movement by people of conscience to change the laws of the states and the nation.

"Declaration of Sentiments"

*We have met together for the achievement of an enterprise, without which that of our **fathers** is incomplete; and which, for its **magnitude, solemnity**, and probable results upon the destiny of the world, as far **transcends** theirs as moral truth does physical force....*

*Their **grievances**, great as they were, were **trifling** in comparison with the wrongs and sufferings of those for whom we plead. Our fathers were never slaves—never bought and sold like cattle—never shut out from the light of knowledge and religion—never subjected to the lash of brutal taskmasters.*

*But those, for whose **emancipation** we are striving—constituting at the present time at least one-sixth part of our countrymen—are recognized by law, and treated by their fellow-beings, as brute beasts; are **plundered** daily of the fruits of their toil without **redress**; really enjoy no **constitutional** nor legal protection from **licentious** and murderous outrages upon their persons; and are ruthlessly torn **asunder**—the tender babe from the arms of its frantic mother—the heartbroken wife from her weeping husband—at the **caprice** or pleasure of irresponsible tyrants. For the crime of having a dark complexion, they suffer the pangs of hunger, the infliction of*

Fathers: Forefathers—i.e., the founding fathers of America.

Magnitude: Greatness.

Solemnity: Seriousness.

Transcends: Rises above.

Grievances: Complaints.

Trifling: Insignificant.

Emancipation: The act of being freed.

Plundered: Robbed.

Redress: The opportunity to make things right.

Constitutional: Referring to the U.S. Constitution, the document which outlines the guiding principles of America's government.

Licentious: Lacking in restraint.

Asunder: Apart.

Caprice: Whim.

Stripes: Lashes from a whip.

Ignominy: Disgrace.

Heathenish darkness: Godless ignorance.

Prominent: Principal or main.

Indisputable: Inarguable.

Civil: Referring to government, or the rights of a citizen under a government.

Piracy: Theft.

In principle: In concept or idea.

Manstealer: Kidnapper.

Pharaoh: Ancient Egyptian kings—one of whom, according to the Bible's Book of Exodus, enslaved the people of Israel.

Entailed: Held, or obligated.

Alienated: Removed.

Risen in solemnity: Increased in seriousness.

An audacious usurpation of the Divine prerogative: An unjustified attempt to take on powers which belong to God.

Infringement: Violation.

Base: Low.

Social compact: The sense of mutual respect and obligation that holds a society together.

Endearments: Bonds of love.

Presumptuous transgression: An unthinking violation.

Abrogated: Repealed or overturned.

stripes, the ***ignominy*** *of brutal servitude. The condition of being a servant or slave.*

*They are kept in **heathenish darkness** by laws expressly enacted to make their instruction a criminal offence.*

*These are the **prominent** circumstances in the condition of more than two million people, the proof of which may be found in thousands of **indisputable** facts, and in the laws of the slaveholding States.*

*Hence we maintain—that, in view of the **civil** and religious privileges of this nation, the guilt of its oppression is unequalled by any other on the face of the earth; and, therefore, that it is bound to repent instantly, to undo the heavy burdens, and to let the oppressed go free....*

*It is **piracy** to buy or steal a native African, and subject him to servitude. Surely, the sin is as great to enslave an American as an African.*

*Therefore we believe and affirm—that there is no difference, **in principle**, between the African slave trade and American slavery:*

*That every American citizen, who detains a human being in involuntary bondage as his property, is, according to Scripture, (Ex. xxi, 16,) a **manstealer:***

That the slaves ought instantly to be set free, and brought under the protection of law:

*That if they had lived from the time of **Pharaoh** down to the present period, and had been **entailed** through successive generations, their right to be free could never have been **alienated**, but their claims would have constantly **risen in solemnity:***

*That all those laws which are now in force, admitting the right of slavery, are therefore, before God, utterly null and void; being **an audacious usurpation of the Divine prerogative**, a daring **infringement** on the law of nature, a **base** overthrow of the very foundations of the **social compact**, a complete extinction of all the relations, **endearments** and obligations of mankind, and a **presumptuous transgression** of all the holy commandments; and that therefore they ought instantly to be **abrogated**.*

We further believe and affirm—that all persons of color, who possess the qualifications which are demanded of others, ought to be admitted forthwith to the enjoyment of the same privileges, and the exercise of the same prerogatives, as others; and that the paths of **preferment**, of wealth and of intelligence, should be opened as widely to them as to persons of a white complexion.

We maintain that no **compensation** should be given to the planters emancipating their slaves:

Because it would be a surrender of the great fundamental principle, that man cannot hold property in man:

Because slavery is a crime, and therefore is not an article to be sold:

Because the holders of slaves are not the **just proprietors** of what they claim; freeing the slave is not depriving them of property, but restoring it to its rightful owner; it is not wronging the master, but righting the slave—restoring him to himself:

Because immediate and general emancipation would only destroy **nominal**, not real property; it would not amputate a limb or break a bone of the slaves, but **by infusing motives into their breasts**, would make them doubly valuable to the masters as free laborers; and

Because, if compensation is to be given at all, it should be given to the outraged and guiltless slaves, and not to those who have plundered and abused them.

We regard as **delusive**, cruel and dangerous, any scheme of **expatriation** which pretends to aid, either directly or indirectly, in the emancipation of the slaves, or to be a substitute for the immediate and total abolition of slavery.

We fully and unanimously recognize the **sovereignty** of each State, to legislate exclusively on the subject of the slavery which is tolerated within its limits; we concede that Congress, under **the present national compact**, has no right to interfere with any of the slave States, in relation to this **momentous** subject:

But we maintain that Congress has a right, and is solemnly bound, to suppress the domestic slave trade between the several States, and to abolish slavery in those portions of our territory which the Constitution has placed under its exclusive **jurisdiction**.

We also maintain that there are, at the present time, the highest obligations resting upon the people of the free States to remove slavery by moral and political action, as prescribed in the Constitution of the United States....

Preferment: Preference or privilege.

Compensation: Repayment.

Just proprietors: Rightful owners.

Nominal: In name only.

By infusing motives into their breasts: In other words, "By giving them a reason to work (because they would be working for themselves.)"

Delusive: Delusional.

Expatriation: Sending a person to another country.

Sovereignty: Right to rule.

The present national compact: Referring to the Constitution.

Momentous: Highly important.

Jurisdiction: Authority.

*These are our views and principles—these our designs and measures. With entire confidence in the overruling justice of God, we plant ourselves upon the Declaration of our Independence and the truths of **Divine Revelation**, as upon **the Everlasting Rock**.*

What happened next...

By 1840, there were more than one hundred antislavery societies in the northern United States; meanwhile, proslavery sentiment in the South became more intense. The federal government again proposed a solution, called the Compromise of 1850. This was a complicated deal for both sides: for instance, it admitted California to the Union as a free state, but it made fugitive, or runaway, slave laws much harsher.

The slavery issue reached a boiling point during the 1850s, with the publication of the highly influential novel *Uncle Tom's Cabin* (1852) by Harriet Beecher Stowe and the adoption of the Kansas-Nebraska Act of 1854. This legislation left open the question of slavery in those two states; this led to the formation of the Republican Party as a powerful force for the antislavery movement.

Disputes over slavery in Kansas and Nebraska led to widespread violence, and this violence would escalate during the decade leading up to the Civil War. In 1859, John Brown (1800–1859) led a daring raid on a federal arms depot in Harper's Ferry, Virginia, hoping to arm slaves for an uprising. He and his followers were hanged. A year later, Abraham Lincoln (1809–1865), running on a clearly antislavery platform or plan of action, became the first Republican President of the United States. Seven slave states withdrew from the Union in protest.

William Lloyd Garrison cofounder of the American Antislavery Society (AAS) and a leading figure in the abolitionist movement played a pivotal role in drafting the AAS Declaration of Sentiments.
Courtesy of The Library of Congress.

Divine Revelation: Wisdom received directly from God.

The Everlasting Rock: God, or God's truth.

William Lloyd Garrison

Cofounder of the American Anti-slavery Society (AAS) and one of the leading figures in the abolitionist movement, William Lloyd Garrison (1805–1879) played a pivotal role in drafting the AAS Declaration of Sentiments. Garrison came from a poor family in Massachusetts, and at age twelve went to work for a local newspaper. By the time he was twenty, he had started his own paper and later went on to become editor of several other publications. It also was during his twenties, that he became involved in the abolitionist movement.

From 1831 to 1865, Garrison edited the *Liberator.* This newspaper was so strong in its antislavery sentiments that after the 1831 slave rebellion led by Nat Turner (1800–1831) was suppressed, many Southern states made it a crime to possess a copy of the paper. In 1833, Garrison helped found the AAS, and served as its president from 1843 to 1865. Garrison's ideas were too extreme for many abolitionists, however: among other things, he called for full equality between blacks and whites, a notion which even the most forward-thinking people of his time considered unsettling.

Following the Civil War (1861–65), which ended slavery, Garrison was an honored man, celebrated among freed slaves and sympathetic whites as a great warrior for freedom. He devoted his latter years to issues such as temperance, or the outlawing of alcohol consumption, and women's rights.

Did you know...

- Sixty-two people signed the American Antislavery Society's Declaration of Sentiments, among them three freed black slaves.

- Despite the fact that the Declaration of Sentiments opposed the idea of creating a homeland in Africa for freed slaves, that was exactly what happened with the establishment of Liberia as a nation in 1847. Liberia's flag resembles that of the United States, and many of its leaders have had American-sounding names such as Doe and Tolbert.

- In his latter years, AAS cofounder William Lloyd Garrison was penniless; however, he managed to live in relative comfort thanks to the generosity of his many supporters.

For more information

Books

Ruchames, Louis, ed. *The Abolitionists: A Collection of Their Writing*. New York: Putnam, 1963.

Sources

Books

Archer, Jules. *Angry Abolitionist: William Lloyd Garrison*. New York: J. Messner, 1969.

Civil War Society. *The American Civil War: A Multicultural Encyclopedia*. Danbury, Conn.: Grolier Educational Corp., 1994.

Faber, Doris. *I Will Be Heard: The Life of William Lloyd Garrison*. New York: Lothrop, Lee and Shepard, 1970.

Lilley, Stephen R. *Fighters Against American Slavery*. San Diego, Calif.: Lucent Books, 1999.

Other

"Abolition." http://members.tripod.com/shanepotter/abolition.html (accessed on May 12, 2000).

"Abolition.html." http://www.germantown.k12.il.us/html/abolition.html (accessed on May 12, 2000).

"Influence of Prominent Abolitionists." *Library of Congress*. http://www.loc.gov/exhibits/african/influ.html (accessed on May 12, 2000).

Anonymous

Excerpt from "A Slave's Story"
Published in *Putnam's Monthly Magazine*, June 1857

By 1857, America was on the brink of civil war. The most significant reason for the conflict was the issue of states' rights—that is, the question of how much power the federal government had over the states. Slavery was related to this issue, as many states wanted to determine for themselves whether they would allow slavery in their state.

Whereas questions regarding federal and state power were largely abstract, or removed from everyday reality, slavery was a highly personal issue. Opponents of slavery sought to make it still more personal through the use of the written word. For example, the 1852 novel *Uncle Tom's Cabin* (1852) by Harriet Beecher Stowe strongly influenced public sentiment against slavery both in the northern United States and in England, whose dependence on cotton from the slaveholding states could otherwise have made it an ally of the South.

But *Uncle Tom's Cabin* was fiction. Much more compelling were the great number of autobiographical slave narratives published in the years leading up to the Civil War (1861–65). The excerpt that follows comes from a long article in the June 1857 issue of *Putnam's Monthly Magazine*. Its au-

I was made, by my parents, the carrier of everything not beyond my strength. I have heard of Indians called Flatheads, because of the shape given to their skulls by pressure. But, if pressure *can* flatten the human head, my race should all be thus deformed; for, in childhood, our heads are the universal vehicles of transportation....

thorship is credited to an anonymous slave, though at places in the narrative, he referred to himself as Ralph. Though Ralph freely acknowledged that his experience is far better than that of most slaves, it is still a tale filled with the painful experiences that characterized the practice of slavery: families separated, children forced to labor, and beatings administered to grown men.

Things to remember while reading

- It should be kept in mind that Ralph's experience was, as he himself wrote, "perhaps, the most pleasant that slavery can exhibit...." Rather than work in the fields, he spent most of his life as a personal attendant to his master or in similar roles. Even a relatively privileged slave such as Ralph, however, had to work in the fields at some point in his life; and Ralph knew enough about the overseer (the white manager of the slaves working in the fields) to avoid him.

- Ralph's narrative may be typical of a slave's attitude toward poor whites. Despite the fact that all whites were technically their social superiors, as Ralph made clear, most slaves looked down on white sharecroppers and others whose station, or position, was hardly better than that of slaves. Indeed, many of the worst conflicts facing freed slaves after the Civil War came not from former plantation owners, but from poor whites jealous of what little the freed slaves possessed.

- A particularly significant theme in Ralph's narrative is the effect of slavery on morality. In a world where parents' children could be taken away, and husbands and wives separated, it was not surprising that Ralph and his first wife Sally treated marriage vows as something of little meaning—or that Ralph considered theft an appropriate means for supporting his family.

- Ralph freely pointed out the extent to which he and those around him had become afflicted with the lowered standards that slavery forced on them, but he was perhaps less aware of the ways he had adopted white peoples' views of slaves. In reference to Sally's willingness to

cheat on her first husband with him, he wrote that "she was not superior to her race or her condition"—meaning that he thought a black slave was capable of no better. He also suggested that what he viewed as Sally's laziness was not merely an outgrowth of slavery, but a condition typical of Africans.

House slaves serving a Southern family dinner. House slaves were considered more privileged than field slaves because housework was not as strenuous as working in the fields.
Reproduced by permission of Corbis Corporation (Bellevue).

"A Slave's Story"

*I was born about the year 1794, on a large plantation, thirty odd miles above Richmond, Virginia, and was descended, in the third generation, from imported Africans, and, probably, from some of the darkest of the native race; for my parents as well as myself were pretty black.... As in most other cases, the **overseer** managed*

Overseer: A white foreman placed in charge of his employer's slaves.

Lunsford Lane

Born in 1803, Lunsford Lane grew up as a slave on a plantation outside of Raleigh, North Carolina. He manufactured pipes, sold tobacco, and raised enough money so that when he was in his thirties, he purchased not only his own freedom, but also that of his wife and seven children.

In 1842, Lane published *The Narrative of Lunsford Lane,* an autobiographical work. In it, he described his first awareness of what it meant to be a slave: "My early boyhood [was spent] in playing with the other boys and girls, colored and white, in the yard, and occasionally doing such little matters of labor as one of so young years could. I knew no difference between myself and the white children; nor did they seem to know any in turn. Sometimes my master would come out and give a biscuit to me, and another to one of his own white boys; but I did not perceive the difference between us....

"When I began to work, I discovered the difference between myself and my master's white children. They began to order me about, and were told to do so by my master and mistress. I found, too, that they had learned to read, while I was not permitted to have a book in my hand. To be in possession of anything written or printed, was regarded as an offence. And then there was the fear that I might be sold away from those who were dear to me, and conveyed to the far South...."

*very well for himself, but not so well for his employer; and, at the death of my parents' master, his debts ... **encumbered** his estate so much, that his only son ... whom I designate as my master, found himself compelled to sell immediately a portion of the slaves. My parents and their five children—including myself, then an infant— were amongst those sold. But their kind master did the best he could for them, and sold the whole family, privately, to some man very near or beyond the mountains. The contrast between their new situation and the mild government of their young master, soon rendered my parents greatly dissatisfied; and, after a few months, they both **absconded** from the purchaser, leaving their four elder children, whom they never saw again, and taking me with them. They found their way back to their former neighborhood, and, for a summer and part of autumn, were concealed in a large body of woods on their former master's premises. Of course, all the neighboring slaves soon knew their lurking place, and supplied them with food, and often with shelter. At length the young master was informed, in some way,*

Encumbered: Tied up.

Absconded: Ran away and hid.

AMERICA

God bless you massa! you feed and clothe us. When we are sick you nurse us, and when too old to work you provide for us!

These poor creatures are a sacred legacy from my ancestors and while a dollar is left me, nothing shall be spared to increase their comfort and happiness.

E.W.C

An engraving showing an idealized Southern belief that plantation owners were willing to provide comfort and happiness to slaves, while slaves were grateful for the care their masters provided for them.
Courtesy of The Library of Congress.

of the circumstance; and, with that kindness which distinguished him through life, he repurchased my parents and myself, at considerable loss and inconvenience....

My earliest recollection of myself is, as a little, black, dirty, un-combed, and unwashed animal, scantily covered with odds and ends of cotton or woolen garments in cool weather, and in the warm season neither having nor desiring any other covering than my own dark skin. And this was universal amongst children, whether male or female, until nine or ten years old. The truth is, the whites in that locality were in a remote situation, at a distance from the frequented roads, and far behind most parts of the state in intelligence and improvement. Raising tobacco was the one sole object in life.... A crop, occupying so much time, and requiring so much attention, compelled both whites and blacks to neglect everything else; and, generally, the former were ignorant and **exacting***, the latter* **debased** *and* **barbarous***, with scarcely a want fully satisfied, and with little more intelligence than the beasts that perish....*

I sat in the ashes, or made dirt-pies in the sand, or hunted for berries or birds' nests, until old enough to carry a pail of water on my head; and then I was made, by my parents, the carrier of everything not beyond my strength. I have heard of Indians called Flatheads, because of the shape given to their skulls by pressure. But, if pressure can flatten the human head, my race should all be thus deformed; for, in childhood, our heads are the universal vehicles of transportation.... A year or two later, I became the carrier of water and food to the hands in the fields; and then was advanced to the post of cow-driver and attendant on the dairy-maid. Now I began to be noticed by my master, and came gradually to be considered in his employment, and began to plow and attend to horses.

My young master, being a bachelor, was much from home; and as soon as I could manage a horse pretty well, I became his attendant—his body-servant, as such were called—on his journeys; he on one horse and I on another, with his **portmanteau***, as large as myself, strapped behind my saddle. I was now in that privileged station, from which I looked down with contempt, not only on most of my own race, but on all poor white folks, as we called all who had not a fair share of property or intelligence. My position as attendant on a gentleman-bachelor of large property, who traveled a good deal, and was at all times kind to his dependents, was, perhaps, the most pleasant that slavery can exhibit.... When at home, I now became the waiter in the house, and a kind of doer of all work about the premises, and, consequently, avoided altogether subjection to the overseer....*

... My master's father had **emancipated** *an elderly negro, named Joe, before such acts were prohibited, and had conveyed to him about sixty acres of land, part of my present master's estate. This old man and his wife now brought from Williamsburg a young female relation named Sally, with her husband and one or two chil-*

Exacting: Petty or small-minded.

Debased: Corrupted.

Barbarous: Behaving like a barbarian, or uncivilized person.

Portmanteau: A large piece of luggage.

Emancipated: Freed.

dren, who were all free. Sally was one of the most beautiful of women. I have never seen one of her color I thought comparable to her. I soon became madly in love. I knew that what is called the marriage tie is usually of little obligation amongst slaves; and that free negroes, being no better taught, if as well, were probably not more virtuous. And how can the slave be expected to observe the marriage vows? In most cases they make none ... [but] have a sort of understanding that their agreement shall continue until one or both choose to form some other tie. And even if wishing to continue

A photo of a typical slave family found on a Southern plantation. This is probably similar to the one that the slave Ralph and his wife Sally raised.
Photograph by T. H. O'Sullivan. Courtesy of The Library of Congress.

Later Slave Narratives

The years leading up to and following the Civil War (1861–1865) saw an increase in the publication of slave narratives. Unlike earlier autobiographical works concerning the capture and enslavement of Africans, these were written by men and women who had grown up as slaves. In rare cases such as that of Ralph in "A Slave's Story," the authors were still enslaved at the time of their writing.

One intriguing postwar slave narrative was "My Escape from Slavery," which appeared in the November 1881 issue of *The Century Illustrated Magazine.* By then, numerous slave narratives had been published. What made this one remarkable was

its author: Frederick Douglass (1817–1895), the most distinguished African American leader of the abolitionist movement.

"In the first narrative of my experience in slavery," Douglass began his account, "and in various writings since, I have given the public what I considered very good reasons for withholding the manner of my escape. In substance these reasons were, first, that such publication at any time during the existence of slavery might be used by the master against the slave, and prevent the future escape of any who might adopt the same means that I did. The second reason was, if possible, still more binding to silence: the publication of details would cer-

faithful unto death, they know their master deems their vows null and void, if he choose to separate them; and he often does thus without **scruple,** *by selling one or both.... I determined, if possible, to get Sally from her husband, and make her my wife; and, after much delay, and more that cannot be told, I found she was not superior to her race or her condition. For a good while, she might be said to have two husbands; but finally her first husband went back, with his own children, to Williamsburg, in company with old Joe, who had sold his land, and Sally became my acknowledged wife. My master strongly disapproved my conduct; but, always kind to the unthankful and the evil, he permitted me, as he did his other men, to build a cabin on the margin of the forest, and thither I carried Sally....*

Sally bore me several children, and in a few years I had a large family to maintain. My wife and children were free, and my master, after giving them a house and patch of ground, fuel, and a supply of meal weekly, and having more than enough of his own slaves to

Scruple: Consideration of ethics or morality.

tainly have put in peril the persons and property of those who assisted [my escape]."

In addition to the autobiographical article, Douglass published several book-length autobiographies. Another well-known late slave narrative was *Up From Slavery* (1901) by Booker T. Washington (1856–1915). Slavery ended when Washington was nine years of age, yet as his autobiography makes clear, emancipation did not end the hardships faced by slaves. They merely exchanged one set of problems for another. Thus he and his brother and stepfather went to work in the furnaces of a salt mine in West Virginia, a very difficult existence.

Describing the conditions his family faced, Washington wrote, "Our new house was no better than the one we had left on the old plantation in Virginia. In fact, in one respect it was worse. Notwithstanding the poor condition of our plantation cabin, we were at all times sure of pure air. Our new home was in the midst of a cluster of cabins crowded closely together, and as there were no sanitary regulations, the filth about the cabins was often intolerable. Some of our neighbours were coloured people, and some were the poorest and most ignorant and degraded white people. It was a motley mixture. Drinking, gambling, quarrels, fights, and shockingly immoral practices were frequent."

*provide for, could not be expected to give them more. Sally, I regret to say, was too much given to **sloth** and **improvidence**—those **plague-spots** inherited from our ancestors, and fostered by our condition here. Most of my time, during the day, being given to my master's interests, necessity compelled me to resort to **expedients**, to which my own **depraved** nature and the example of other slaves already tempted me....*

What happened next...

Ralph's narrative continued at some length, describing the ways he supplemented his income through theft and the punishments he suffered. He regarded Sally's death, which

Sloth: Laziness.

Improvidence: Lack of concern for, or awareness of, the future.

Plague-spots: Weaknesses.

Expedients: Solutions, or short cuts.

Depraved: Lacking in morality.

came suddenly and prematurely, as another form of punishment against him—this one from God—for taking her from her husband. He sent his children away to be raised by others, and after some time, he married again. His happiness was cut short when his master sold him to a new owner. He escaped and returned to the home of his old master (actually, the master's son, now head of the household), who welcomed him back.

It was this man who sent Ralph's lengthy autobiography to *Putnam's* not long after the slave died at age sixty-three. Along with it, the white man included the following note: "The slave question is becoming more and more prominent, and I have thought it well to give a simple, faithful narrative of a slave's experience and views. The sketch has not been gotten up for effect, but has been written as an authentic illustration of the results, moral and physical, of the [slave] system. Though the owner of slaves, I have always advocated some plan of gradual emancipation *by our own state,* and, therefore, have no motive for concealing anything in relation to the effects of slavery. I have given, exactly, Ralph's narrative—many facts I could myself establish, and verify others by unquestionable evidence."

The family that "owned" Ralph at the beginning and end of his life was highly unusual among Southern slaveholders. Presumably it was under the guidance of this family that Ralph learned how to read and write, though Ralph never mentions the fact, no doubt because it was illegal to teach reading and writing to a slave. Despite the misfortunes he encountered with this family, and the fact that he and others were bought and sold several times, life could have been much, much worse, and indeed it was for most slaves.

Did you know...

- *Putnam's Monthly Magazine* was owned by G. P. Putnam, who founded the publishing company G. P. Putnam & Son in 1866. Nearly 140 years later, as a vast conglomerate called the Berkley Putnam Group, it remains one of America's leading publishers.

- One of the most famous short stories by Herman Melville (1819–1891), best-known for his masterpiece *Moby Dick*

(1851), was "Bartleby, the Scrivener: A Story of Wall-Street." The story was first published, anonymously, in the November and December 1853 issues of *Putnam's Monthly Magazine*.

For more information

Periodicals

Anonymous. "A Slave's Story." *Putnam's Monthly Magazine,* Vol. 9, June, 1857, pp. 614–20.

Sources

Books

Andrews, William L. and Henry Louis Gates Jr., eds. *The Civitas Anthology of African American Slave Narratives.* Washington, D.C.: Civitas/Counterpoint, 1999.

Douglass, Frederick. *Escape from Slavery: The Boyhood of Frederick Douglass in His Own Words.* Edited and illustrated by Michael McCurdy, foreword by Coretta Scott King. New York: Knopf, 1994.

Lane, Lunsford. *The Narrative of Lunsford Lane, Formerly of Raleigh, N.C., Embracing an Account of His Early Life, the Redemption by Purchase of Himself and Family from Slavery, and His Banishment from the Place of His Birth for the Crime of Wearing a Colored Skin; Published by Himself.* Boston: Hewes and Watson, 1845.

Taylor, Yuval, ed. *I Was Born a Slave: An Anthology of Classic Slave Narratives.* Chicago: Lawrence Hill Books, 1999.

Washington, Booker T. *Up from Slavery; and Other Early Black Narratives.* New York: Doubleday, 1998.

Other

"A Slave's Story." *Electronic Text Center, University of Virginia Library.* http://extext.lib.virginia.edu/etcbin/browsemixednew?id=AnoSlav&images=images/modeng&data=/texts/english/modeng/parsed&tag=public (accessed on May 12, 2000).

Abraham Lincoln

Emancipation Proclamation
Reprinted in *The American Revolution—an .HTML project*, 1997

United States Constitution

Amendments 13 to 15
Reprinted in *DISCovering World History*, 2000

By the 1860 presidential elections, tensions in America had reached a boiling point. The Democratic Party had divided into proslavery and antislavery factions while the Republican Party, united in its opposition to slavery, nominated Abraham Lincoln (1809–1865) for president. Lincoln, who opposed both the spread of slavery and efforts by government to forcibly end it, won the November presidential elections.

Lincoln's victory sparked enormous hostility in the South, where slaveholders feared that the federal government would take their "property"; therefore, a group of Southern leaders met to form a breakaway government, the Confederate States of America. South Carolina was the first state to secede, or separate itself, from the United States, and ten others followed: Alabama, Arkansas, Florida, Georgia, Louisiana, Mississippi, North Carolina, Tennessee, Texas, and Virginia. The Confederacy also claimed two other states, Missouri and Kentucky, for a total of thirteen, a number intended to reflect that of America's thirteen original colonies. However, Missouri and Kentucky never actually seceded, and though both allowed slavery, they were actually part of the Union.

... nor shall any State deprive any person of life, liberty, or property, without due process of law....

From the United States Constitution, Amendment 14, Section 1

Armed hostilities began on April 12, 1861, when Confederate forces opened fire on the federal installation at Fort Sumter, which was located in the harbor of Charleston, South Carolina. Initially the war seemed to favor the Confederacy, which had superior generals, and the South gained a number of victories in the first year of the war.

Lincoln had long insisted that the purpose of the war was to preserve the Union, but pressure from a number of sides, most notably from abolitionist leaders, forced him to place a greater emphasis on freeing the slaves. In July 1862 he drafted a preliminary version of the Emancipation Proclamation, which freed all slaves in the Confederate states as of January 1, 1863. His cabinet, or the presidential advisors, suggested that he not make the proclamation public until the Union had secured a major victory in battle; otherwise, it might appear like a desperate ploy to gain support from antislavery elements.

This major victory came in September, at the Battle of Antietam in Maryland. Soon afterward, Lincoln issued the Emancipation Proclamation. This document only freed the slaves in the Confederate states, however, and it became increasingly clear that after a Union victory, *all* the slaves in the United States would have to be freed. To do so, and to ensure that slavery would never again be legal in the United States, required a constitutional amendment. Congress passed three significant amendments after the war: the Thirteenth, which ended slavery; the Fourteenth, which granted slaves citizenship; and the Fifteenth, which made them eligible to vote.

Things to remember while reading

- The Emancipation Proclamation was an order from the executive branch of the United States government and, therefore, did not need the approval of Congress. By contrast, a constitutional amendment, that is, a change to the Constitution, the central document guiding the government, requires a vote of Congress, or the legislative branch. The judicial branch of the government would be the testing ground for the amendments as participants in lawsuits brought legal challenges (particularly ones concerning the Fourteenth Amendment) before the Supreme Court.

It should be stressed that the Emancipation Proclamation only freed slaves in the South. Thus, for the remainder of the war, slavery continued in Kentucky, Missouri, and other non-Confederate states where slavery was still legal. The document's greatest significance was that it legally freed Southern slaves to leave their masters and enlist in the Union army.

- The Civil War Amendments, as the Thirteenth, Fourteenth, and Fifteenth amendments are called, strongly reflect the time in which they were written. Today people refer to "the United States" as a single entity, but this was not customary until after the Civil War. Thus, the Thirteenth Amendment, drafted just after the war, still uses *their* rather than *its* as a possessive pronoun referring to the United States.

- By the time of the Emancipation Proclamation, the Confederacy as a whole remained defiant. Five years later,

Abraham Lincoln (third from the left) at the first reading of the Emancipation Proclamation.
Courtesy of The Library of Congress.

when the Fourteenth Amendment was adopted, quite a different situation prevailed: the war was over, the Confederacy destroyed, and former opponents of the United States wanted to return to the rights they had previously enjoyed under the federal government. The Union did not make this easy, however. States had to apply for readmission to the Union; and many individuals never regained the rights they had enjoyed before the war. In fact, much of the Fourteenth Amendment concerns persons who had served the Confederacy: as punishment for their part in the rebellion, most of these individuals would not enjoy full civil rights under the restored Union.

The Emancipation Proclamation

By the President of the United States of America:

A PROCLAMATION

*Whereas on the 22nd day of September, A.D. 1862, a proclamation was issued by the President of the United States, containing, among other things, the following, **to wit:***

*"That on the 1st day of January, A.D. 1863, all persons held as slaves within any State or designated part of a State the people whereof shall then be in rebellion against the United States shall be then, thenceforward, and forever free; and the **executive government** of the United States, including the military and naval authority thereof, will recognize and maintain the freedom of such persons and will do no act or acts to repress such persons, or any of them, in any efforts they may make for their actual freedom.*

*"That the executive will on the 1st day of January **aforesaid**, by proclamation, designate the States and parts of States, if any, in which the people thereof, respectively, shall then be in rebellion against the United States; and the fact that any State or the people thereof shall on that day be in good faith represented in the Congress of the United States by members chosen thereto at elections wherein a majority of the qualified voters of such States shall have participated shall, in the absence of strong **countervailing** testimo-*

To wit: Namely, or specifically.

Executive government: The executive branch of the government, headed by the president.

Aforesaid: As said before

Countervailing: Counteracting or opposing.

ny, be deemed conclusive evidence that such State and the people thereof are not then in rebellion against the United States."

Now, therefore, I, Abraham Lincoln, President of the United States, by virtue of the power in me vested as Commander-In-Chief of the Army and Navy of the United States in time of actual armed rebellion against the authority and government of the United States, and as a fit and necessary war measure for suppressing said rebellion, do, on this 1st day of January, A.D. 1863, and in accordance with my purpose so to do, publicly proclaim for the full period of one hundred days from the first day above mentioned, order and designate as the States and parts of States wherein the people thereof, respectively, are this day in rebellion against the United States the following, to wit:

*Arkansas, Texas, Louisiana (except the **parishes** of St. Bernard, Palquemines, Jefferson, St. John, St. Charles, St. James, Ascension, Assumption, Terrebone, Lafourche, St. Mary, St. Martin, and Orleans, including the city of New Orleans), Mississippi, Alabama, Florida, Georgia, South Carolina, North Carolina, and Virginia (except the forty-eight counties designated as West Virginia, and also the counties of Berkeley, Accomac, Northhampton, Elizabeth City, York, Princess Anne, and Norfolk, including the cities of Norfolk and Portsmouth), and which excepted parts are for the present left precisely as if this proclamation were not issued.*

And by virtue of the power and for the purpose aforesaid, I do order and declare that all persons held as slaves within said designated States and parts of States are, and henceforward shall be, free; and that the Executive Government of the United States, including the military and naval authorities thereof, will recognize and maintain the freedom of said persons.

*And I hereby enjoin upon the **people** so declared to be free to abstain from all violence, unless in necessary self-defence; and I recommend to them that, in all case when allowed, they labor faithfully for reasonable wages.*

*And I further declare and make known that such persons of suitable condition will be received into the armed service of the United States to **garrison** forts, positions, stations, and other places, and to man vessels of all sorts in said service.*

And upon this act, sincerely believed to be an act of justice, warranted by the Constitution upon military necessity, I invoke the considerate judgment of mankind and the gracious favor of Almighty God.

Parishes: The equivalent of counties in Louisiana.

People: In this case, slaves.

Garrison: To occupy with troops.

Abraham Lincoln

Born in a log cabin in Hardin County, Kentucky, on February 12, 1809, Abraham Lincoln was close to his mother as a child. After her death, he was raised by his sister Sarah. Lincoln did not enjoy a close relationship with his father, who did little to foster the young man's education. Nevertheless, Lincoln set out to educate himself, walking long miles to a library where he could borrow books and reading them by candlelight.

When Lincoln was nineteen, Sarah died. Soon afterward, he took the first of two significant trips down the Mississippi River, working on a "flatboat" carrying cargo. In 1831, he made his second flatboat journey, and the exposure to new places greatly broadened his mind. After his second trip, he settled in Illinois and volunteered in the Black Hawk War, a conflict with local Native Americans.

In 1832 the twenty-three-year-old Lincoln ran unsuccessfully for the Illinois state legislature. This was followed by a short and disastrous career in business, after which Lincoln worked briefly as a postmaster and deputy surveyor. It was not a promising beginning for a man who would one day become one of his nation's greatest leaders. Yet he won election to the state legislature in 1834, and by teaching himself law was able to earn a license to practice it in 1836. He moved to Springfield, the state capital in 1837, and gained prominence in a number of federal court cases around the area.

In his early thirties, Lincoln fell in love with Mary Todd, a spirited and popular young woman whose manner contrasted sharply with Lincoln's shy, sometimes awkward ways. The two were married on November 4, 1842, and had four sons, only one of whom would live past his teen

United States Constitution

Amendment XIII
December 18, 1865
Section 1

Neither slavery nor involuntary servitude, except as a punishment for crime whereof the party shall have been duly convicted, shall exist within the United States, or any place subject to their jurisdiction.

years. Lincoln went on to serve in the U.S. House of Representatives for one term (1847–49), and ran unsuccessfully for the Senate in 1855. By 1856, Lincoln had switched his allegiance from the disintegrating Whig Party to the new Republican Party, which was strongly antislavery.

Lincoln's fame grew when he ran against Democrat Stephen Douglas for Douglas's Senate seat in 1858. He did not win, but a series of Lincoln-Douglas debates gained national attention because of the candidates' fiery discussions on the issues of slavery expansion in the United States. Then in May 1860, Lincoln unexpectedly won the Republican nomination as their presidential candidate. Due to nationwide disagreement over slavery, the presidential race was split between four candidates. This helped Lincoln to a surprise win in the November elections.

In April 1861, a month after Lincoln was sworn in as president, the Civil War began. It would occupy virtually all of his attention for the remainder of his administration. After initial Confederate victories, the tide of the war began to turn in 1862; Union victories at Vicksburg, Mississippi and Gettysburg, Virginia in 1863 helped seal the fate of the Confederacy. Yet the war dragged on through 1864, which saw the destruction of Atlanta—a decisive blow to the Confederacy—and Lincoln's reelection. Finally, on April 9, 1865, Confederate forces surrendered. Lincoln, often criticized as much by his own side as by the Confederacy, was now widely praised. Unfortunately, he did not have long to enjoy his success: five days after the surrender, on April 14, 1865, Lincoln was assassinated by John Wilkes Booth while viewing a performance at Ford's Theatre in Washington, D.C.

Section 2

Congress shall have power to enforce this article by appropriate legislation.

Amendment XIV
July 28, 1868
Section 1

*All persons born or **naturalized** in the United States, and subject to the jurisdiction thereof, are citizens of the United States and of the State wherein they reside. No State shall make or enforce any law which shall **abridge** the privileges or **immunities** of citizens of the United States; nor shall any State deprive any person of life, lib-*

Naturalized: To become citizens of a country.

Abridge: Reduce.

Immunities: Freedoms.

erty, or property, without due process of law; nor deny to any person within its jurisdiction the equal protection of the laws.

Section 2

Representatives shall be **apportioned** among the several States according to their respective numbers, counting the whole number of persons in each State, excluding Indians not taxed. But when the right to vote at any election for the choice of **electors** for President and Vice President of the United States, Representatives in Congress, the Executive and Judicial officers of a State, or the members of the Legislature thereof, is denied to any of the male inhabitants of such State, being twenty-one years of age, and citizens of the United States, or in any way abridged, except for participation in rebellion, or other crime, the basis of representation therein shall be reduced in the proportion which the number of such male citizens shall bear to the whole number of male citizens twenty-one years of age in such State.

Section 3

No person shall be a Senator or Representative in Congress, or elector of President and Vice President, or hold any office, civil or military, under the United States, or under any State, who, having previously taken an oath, as a member of Congress, or as an officer of the United States, or as a member of any State legislature, or as an executive or judicial officer of any State, to support the Constitution of the United States, shall have engaged in insurrection or rebellion against the same, or given aid or comfort to the enemies thereof. But Congress may by a vote of two-thirds of each House, remove such disability.

Section 4

The validity of the public debt of the United States, authorized by law, including debts incurred for payment of pensions and bounties for services in suppressing insurrection or rebellion, shall not be questioned. But neither the United States nor any State shall assume or pay any debt or obligation incurred in aid of insurrection or rebellion against the United States, or any claim for the loss or emancipation of any slave; but all such debts, obligations and claims shall be held illegal and void.

Section 5

The Congress shall have power to enforce, by appropriate legislation, the provisions of this article.

Apportioned: Distributed proportionately according to a plan.

Electors: Members of the electoral college, a group of delegates whose votes officially elect the U.S. president and vice president.

Amendment XV
March 30, 1870
Section 1

The right of citizens of the United States to vote shall not be denied or abridged by the United States or by any State on account of race, color, or previous condition of servitude.

Section 2

The Congress shall have power to enforce this article by appropriate legislation.

What happened next...

Along with the victory at Antietam, and those at Vicksburg and Gettysburg that followed, the Emancipation Proclamation marked a turning point in the Civil War. No longer was the war simply about the preservation of the Union; with the document, it became a fight for freedom. Awareness of this moral purpose gave renewed energy to the Union's military effort, and the proclamation opened the floodgates for enlistment by former slaves. By war's end, some 180,000 African American men had served in the Union forces.

The Civil War Amendments officially ended slavery and, in theory, secured the civil rights of African Americans. The Fifth Amendment, adopted long before, had guaranteed citizens' right to "due process of law"—for example, a fair trial—but the Fourteenth Amendment took the crucial step of applying this federal provision to the states. In future years, many segments of society would invoke the Fourteenth Amendment to guarantee their constitutional rights.

Unfortunately, laws could only do so much to change conditions. In many cases, African Americans found that they were only slightly better off after slavery than they had been under it. Much of this was due to the inept manner in which the federal government handled the difficult period after the war known as Reconstruction (1865–77), its effort to enforce rapid change in the South. By eliminating the civil rights of

Emancipation of the Serfs

By the mid-1800s, the system of serfdom had long since died out in Western Europe, but not in Russia. In fact, progress seemed to move from the West to the East, with Britain becoming the first major nation to abolish all forms of slavery, serfdom, and indentured servitude. Meanwhile, far to the east, Russia held on to their old traditions regarding serfdom.

The vast majority of Russian people were either serfs or poor peasants. What distinguished serfs from ordinary peasants was not necessarily the quality of life—peasants hardly had an easy existence—but the fact that a serf was tied to the estate where he or she lived, and to the master who "owned" him or her. At the opposite end of Russian society was a wealthy and well-educated elite who enjoyed a privileged existence.

As in America and Brazil, where plantation owners "needed" slaves to work large tracts of land, the sheer size of Russia had virtually forced serfdom into being. What sustained serfdom, however, was the power of the czars, Russia's iron-fisted emperors. By the 1800s, however, an educated segment of the upper class had begun to question not only the absolute power of the czars, but also the virtual enslavement of the population under serfdom.

Among this educated group was Prince Peter Kropotkin (1842–1921), a member of a radical political faction who

Southerners and virtually guaranteeing the election of black legislators, the government embittered the white power structure of the South. With the removal of federal troops in 1877, Southerners were free to treat the black people in their states as they pleased, and this led to an erosion of the rights established in the Civil War Amendments. Only with the gains made by the Civil Rights movement of the 1950s and 1960s would blacks begin to enjoy the full rights of U.S. citizenship.

Did you know...

- The stars on the Confederate battle flag, or "stars and bars," stood for the thirteen states of the Confederacy. Nearly a century later, during the civil rights struggles of the 1950s, the flag gained new meaning as white opponents of racial integration adopted it as a symbol. By the

later wrote about his father's treatment of his serfs. Displeased with one of his servants, Kropotkin's father ordered that the servant receive "A hundred lashes with the birch rod" at the local police station. Yet as Kropotkin went on to note, "father was not among the worst of the landowners. On the contrary, the servants and the peasants considered him one of the best. What we saw in our house was going on everywhere, often in much more cruel forms. The flogging of the serfs was a regular part of the duties of the police and the fire brigade."

The coronation of Czar Alexander II (1818–1881) in 1855 signaled the beginnings of change. Alexander, probably the most liberal czar Russia ever had, wanted to reform the system. Two years before Lincoln's Emancipation Proclamation in 1863, Alexander emancipated the serfs. The Russian serf population was actually much larger than the slave population in the United States. However, unlike the Americans, the Russians did not have to fight a war to free them.

Unfortunately, the pace of reform under Alexander was not fast enough for some political groups, and one of these groups assassinated the czar in 1881. The situation of the serfs, as it turned out, was similar to that of the slaves in the United States: emancipation did little to change their actual situation. Problems in Russia continued to fester, and in 1917 they would erupt leading to the Russian Revolution.

1990s, numerous civil rights groups opposed display of the flag, which they equated with slavery and white supremacy.

- If the Constitution had a list of "greatest hits," the Fourteenth Amendment would be on it. The U.S. Supreme Court has reviewed few cases concerning the Third Amendment, for instance, which protects citizens from being forced to provide lodging for troops in peacetime. By contrast, the Fourteenth Amendment's provision concerning "due process of law" is one of the most invoked phrases in constitutional law.

- One of American history's great ironies concerns Confederate General Robert E. Lee and Union General Ulysses S. Grant, respectively the commanders of the Confederate and Union forces in the Civil War. A Virginian loyal to his state, Lee sided with the Confederacy, yet freed his slaves as soon as the war began, to show that he was not fighting for personal gain. By contrast, Grant (who later served two terms as U.S. president) owned four slaves.

For more information

Books

Burchard, Peter. *Lincoln and Slavery.* New York: Atheneum Books for Young Readers, 1999.

Carey, Charles W., Jr. *The Emancipation Proclamation.* Chanhassen, Minn.: Child's World, 2000.

Henry, Christopher E. *Forever Free: From the Emancipation Proclamation to the Civil Rights Bill of 1875, 1863–1875.* New York: Chelsea House, 1995.

Schleichert, Elizabeth. *The Thirteenth Amendment: Ending Slavery.* Springfield, N.J.: Enslow Publishers, 1998.

Wade, Linda R. *Reconstruction: The Years Following the Civil War.* Edina, Minn.: Abdo & Daughters, 1998.

Other

The Civil War (documentary; nine episodes). Warner Home Video, 1990.

"Civil War Resources on the Internet: Abolitionism to Reconstruction." *Rutgers University Library.* http://www.libraries.rutgers.edu/rulib/socsci/hist/civwar2.html (accessed on May 12, 2000).

Late Modern Slavery
(1900–Present)

3

S lavery in the twentieth century would take on a variety of new forms, and would in many instances prove more gruesome than anything that preceded it. As cruel as slavery had been in the American South during the nineteenth century, for instance, few slaveholders had tried to work their slaves to death, if for no other reason that they considered them valuable "property." In the twentieth century, however, slave-labor camps in Germany, the Soviet Union (a former country of eastern Europe and northern Asia that united Russia and various other soviet republics), China, and other nations became death camps.

Slavery in modern times, particularly slavery that was politically motivated, truly took shape in the latter part of World War I (1914–18). By that time, Germany was having difficulty maintaining its war effort against Britain, France, Russia, and their allies, and needed to produce more weapons and ammunition. To that end the German military began using large brigades of captured civilians for labor in munitions factories. Although using prisoners as a work force does not necessarily constitute slavery, the conditions im-

Soviet dictator Joseph Stalin built his regime on slave labor, repression, death.
Reproduced by permission of UPI/Corbis-Bettmann.

posed by the Germans, combined with the fact that those imprisoned were typically neither criminals nor combatants, makes this the first notable use of slave labor in the twentieth century.

German methods deeply impressed a young Russian Marxist (see sidebar, "Marxism and Slavery") named V. I. Lenin (1870–1924). At one time Russia had a large numbers of serfs (peasants who work the land for a lord), but the Russian government had abolished serfdom in 1861. Yet in 1917, Lenin and his political party, the Bolsheviks, seized control. Lenin employed these slave-labor methods employed by the Germans, and also those once used in Russia by the old imperial government. Slave labor in the Soviet Union would further expand under Lenin's successor, Joseph Stalin (1879–1953), who ruled for a quarter-century beginning in the late 1920s.

Soviet Communism (a system of government in which the state plans and controls the economy and a single, often authoritarian state) was one type of totalitarianism. Another was Nazism, which took hold in Germany in 1933 under the control of Adolf Hitler (1889–1945). Totalitarian systems demand that people submit completely to the state, or the government. These governments maintain their power through secret police, prisons, and concentration camps, which are huge facilities for political or war prisoners. Another common feature of totalitarian states is the implementation of enormous projects: road building, dam construction, and other large construction projects.

Given all these conditions, the use of slave labor was almost inevitable, not only in Soviet Russia but also in Nazi Germany. With the advent of World War II (1939–45), the Nazis forced captured combatants and civilians in enemy countries to act as slave labor. Among these was **Aimé Boni-**

fas, a future pastor who took part in antigovernment activities in German-occupied France in 1940.

During World War II, the Nazis were allied with the Japanese, whose government was highly militarized and had a low regard for human life. Just how low that regard was is illustrated by the story of the "comfort woman" **Yun Turi.** "Comfort women" were non-Japanese women (primarily Koreans) forced into prostitution as a means of satisfying the needs of Japanese soldiers, in other words, they were sex slaves, a type of slave that had hardly existed prior to the twentieth century.

By mid-century, it was clear that slavery had returned with a vengeance, in forms and on a scale hardly imagined by previous generations. Though Germany and Japan were defeated in World War II, and as a result were forced to adopt new forms of government, there was one country that found a way to maintain its slave-labor system: the Soviet Union. Once allies with the United States and Britain during World War II, the Soviet Union became a formidable enemy of the both countries during a period known as the Cold War (a period beginning after World War II in which conditions of hostility and military build-up short of actual armed conflict lasting until 1989).

As the **American Federation of Labor** noted in a 1947 statement, the Soviet system was the greatest threat to freedom in the world. Soon after that statement, communism took hold in China under Mao Zedong (1893–1976), who ruled that country for more than thirty years and imprisoned, enslaved, and murdered millions of his countrymen.

An admirer of Stalin, Mao adopted an extreme version of Marxism (the political and economic ideas of Karl Marx and Friedrich Engels on which Soviet Communism was based) while the Soviet system became less brutal in the years following Stalin's death. Among Mao's admirers was a group called the Khmer Rouge, or "Red Cambodians." From 1975 to 1979 the Khmer Rouge forced millions of Cambodians into a brutal form of slave labor. During this time, the outside world was largely ignorant of the crimes committed by the Khmer Rouge. Later, however, the full story was revealed, partly through the efforts of individuals such as **François Ponchaud,** a French priest who reported information he had learned from Cambodian survivors.

By the end of the twentieth century, the horrors of totalitarianism in Cambodia and most other countries were a thing of the past, thanks in large part to the downfall of Soviet Communism in the late 1980s and early 1990s. But slavery continued to exist in a variety of forms, as articles by **Huw Watkin**, **Vijay Prashad**, and the **All Africa News Agency**, all published in the last few months of 1999, all illustrate.

Not only was there still political slavery in some countries, there was sex slavery, as reported by Watkin; in addition, child labor still flourished in some parts of the world, which was the subject of Prashad's article. To top it off, old-fashioned chattel slavery, in particular, the traffic in human beings captured from Africa, still existed, as the All Africa News Agency and others made clear.

Some sources estimated that at the end of the twentieth century, more people were enslaved than ever before. For instance, it was estimated that 25,000,000 children were enslaved and forced into child labor. It is clear that the world still had a long, long way to go to rid itself from slavery.

Aimé Bonifas

Excerpt from **Prisoner 20–801:**
A French National in the Nazi Labor Camps
Published in *Prisoner 20–801:*
***A French National in the Nazi Labor Camps*, 1987**

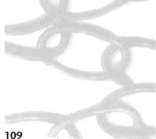

By the time Aimé Bonifas was imprisoned by the Germans, slavery had long since been revived in its twentieth-century forms. This had been aided by the spread of totalitarian systems, (totalitarian systems demand that people submit completely to the state, or the government) most notably Marxism (the political and economic ideas of Karl Marx and Friedrich Engels on which Soviet Communism was based) and Nazism (the ideology and practice of the Nazis, especially the policy of racist nationalism, national expansion, and state control of the economy) in Germany.

Led by Adolf Hitler (1889–1945), the Nazis had taken over the German government in 1933. Once in power, they dealt harshly with enemies both real (i.e. communists and members of other political parties) and those they imagined to be their enemies. In fact, their most brutal treatment was toward groups such as Gypsies, homosexuals, and Jews, who could not possibly have posed a serious threat to the Nazi government.

In twelve years, the Nazis imprisoned and murdered millions of Jews, Gypsies, homosexuals, Jehovah's Witnesses

I had observed that some prisoners—poor intimidated fellows, robots of the System—killed themselves with work when they could have limited their output. We marked them well, for by increasing production norms, they involuntarily became our enemies.

Marxism and Slavery

Communism, the system of government that prevailed in the Soviet Union and other countries during much of the twentieth century, is more accurately known as Marxism, or better yet, Marxism Leninism. In theory, it is a system in which the people jointly own all property; but in practice, Marxist-Leninist governments control not only all property, but virtually all other aspects of life. During the twentieth century, millions and millions of people worked and died in slave-labor camps operated by Marxist-Leninist regimes in Eastern Europe, East Asia, Africa, and Latin America.

It is ironic that Marxism, the creation of German philosophers Karl Marx (1818–1883) and Friedrich Engels (1820–1895), would become the justification for the enslavement of millions. Marx and Engels predicted that nineteenth-century wage-slavery, a situation in which factory owners profited from the labor of workers, would come to an end. The workers would seize control of the factories and share in the wealth of their production. Justice and equality would reign supreme, according to Marx and Engels.

Historians have often disputed the degree to which Marx and Engels were responsible for the horrors of Soviet Communism. Yet their writings did little to explain *how* the workers would seize control. In their view, this would simply happen, and it would take place in the most economically advanced countries, such as Britain, first.

The Russian Marxist V. I. Lenin (1870–1924), however, knew exactly how to take power: by force. With help from the Germans, who rightly believed that Lenin would topple the Russian government and

and other innocent people. In some cases the Nazis simply killed their victims in gas chambers (sealed rooms filled with poisonous gas); but more often these prisoners were used for slave labor before being killed. Much of this took place during World War II, when the Nazis took advantage of the confusion brought on by the war. It was at this time that they developed what they named "the Final Solution" to the Jewish problem, the complete extermination of the Jews, now know as the Holocaust.

The Holocaust is a subject unto itself, and due to the sheer enormity of that crime, German use of non-Jewish slave labor has received less attention. On June 22, 1941, Nazi Germany invaded the Soviet Union (a former

withdraw his country's troops from World War I, Lenin and his tiny political power seized control in November 1917. Russia was far from an economically advanced country, but Lenin maintained that by employing ruthless means, his government could achieve the goals outlined by Marx and Engels. This ultimately became a justification for slave labor. Not only was it justifiable to arrest, imprison, and enslave people who had benefited from the pre-Marxist system, but Lenin considered such measures appropriate for anyone who dared criticize his party's leadership.

Lenin's successor, Joseph Stalin (1879–1953), greatly expanded the Marxist system developed by Lenin, using huge slave-labor brigades to build railroads and dams and to mine resources ranging from salt to gold. Millions died in Stalin's slave-labor camps. The Russian writer Aleksandr Solzhenitsyn (1918–) and others exposed the brutality of the Stalinist system, yet Stalin's and Lenin's interpretation of Marxism spread to other countries.

Hitler's Nazism attracted far more attention because of its racist character, but in fact Marxism killed far more people. (As a matter of fact, Hitler and other Nazis were influenced by Marxist ideas, which they simply reinterpreted in racial terms.)

During the late 1980s and early 1990s, the Soviet Union and a number of other countries rejected Marxist Leninism, but it would take many years to overcome the effects of totalitarianism. At the beginning of the twenty-first century, only a handful of countries, primarily China, Cuba, and North Korea, maintained Marxist systems. All are noted for their use of slave labor.

country of eastern Europe and northern Asia that united Russia and various other soviet republics), breaking a two-year alliance between the two nations. In the months and years that followed, the Nazis enslaved huge numbers of Russians and other Soviet citizens many of which were Jewish. According to the Nazis' beliefs, Jews were less than human and the people of Eastern Europe were only slightly better. This was the justification for their brutal treatment of people in that region.

By contrast, the Nazis were far less cruel to the citizens of nations they conquered to the north and west of Germany, including France, which they subdued in June 1940. Aimé Bonifas, a French citizen born in 1920, might never have been interned in a Nazi concentration camp; however, he took part in anti-Nazi activities, aided the French Resistance, and tried to escape from Nazi-controlled France. Following his capture, he was interned in a number of camps, including the forced-labor camp at Mackenrode, where events in the following passage took place.

Things to remember while reading

- Bonifas's experience was not as horrible as that of the approximate six million Jews murdered in Nazi death camps, nor of the millions other people also murdered by the Nazis. Thus his account illustrates the brutality with which the Nazis treated even people who were not part of targeted group such as Jews, Gypsies, or homosexuals.

- The "Laura" referred to by Bonifas was not a woman, but a camp where he and others had been confined. Like the more well-known Auschwitz, Laura was an extermination camp. Hence his comment that "To remain at Laura had promised nothing."

- As Bonifas made clear, in a situation of forced labor it was best to work just enough to keep from being harmed. Those prisoners who showed too much enthusiasm and worked harder than was necessary simply increased the expectations on the whole group, which explains his comment about prisoners who worked too hard: "We marked them well, for by increasing production norms, they involuntarily became our enemies."

- Bonifas provides an inside view of the black market, or illegal trade in goods. Because they were always underfed and overworked, the prisoners were eager to buy or trade illegally for food and other "luxuries."

Prisoner 20-801

*Under a hail of punches and kicks, we learned the technology by which ancient slaves constructed **grandiose** works. We slid **studs***

Grandiose: Absurdly grand or splendid.

Studs: Boards.

under the trunk, and two of us on each side of the trunk grasped each stud. We placed the studs as closely as our ranks would permit. Fifty or sixty men could hoist the tree and carry it to the designated location. What an effort! This task demanded tremendous muscular exertion. The tall inmates, of whom I was one, were at a disadvantage. They bore the brunt of the burden for the short inmates and for those who only pretended to exert themselves. No sooner had we put down the first trunk than we had to hoist the second. There was no time to catch our breath or to talk about a better procedure. Indeed, the **kapo** found that there were too many of us for a single trunk and that the work did not progress quickly enough; therefore, he divided us into two teams. At first, we had carried the trees that were at hand or that were the smallest. Thus, at last, when we were drained of our strength, the heaviest trunks were still to be moved. In the afternoon, we were ordered to lift trunks that had fallen on marshy ground. Slipping and panting all the while, we risked dropping the trunk and breaking the legs of all the men on one side of it. The superhuman task was all the more difficult to perform because we were weakened by months of **malnutrition**. Our foreman was an irresponsible gypsy type, an impostor who seemed to find a sadistic pleasure in making us suffer.

Once again we had to ascend **Calvary** as the grimmest days overshadowed us. Surely, such **duress** would not last forever, but, in the meantime, we had to survive. My back ached, my arm and leg muscles knotted, and I was dizzy. My comrades were also spent. And always, **"Los, los, schneller,"** with no letup! Indeed, we exercised our will until our will was broken. But every day had an evening. At the close of the workday, each of us lugged back to the camp a chunk for the kitchen fire. We literally dragged ourselves to the compound.

This routine was followed every day. Some Frenchmen who had been in this **commando** for a month were completely exhausted. The rest of us, like them, would not be able to endure. Many regretted ever having left Laura. For me, it seemed that there was nothing to regret. To remain at Laura had promised nothing. Now, without looking back, we should courageously accept our fate.

We were laying the roadbed for a new railway. We were urged on because the approaching winter freezes might hamper or interrupt our work. It seemed that this railroad was of some military significance....

One way or the other, the work proceeded. A new commando, number 16, was formed, and I was assigned to it. Each morning we

Kapo: Supervisor or gang-boss.

Malnutrition: The result of being inadequately fed over an extended period.

Calvary: The hill near Jerusalem where Jesus Christ was crucified. Here the term is used symbolically.

Duress: Captivity

Los, los, schneller: German for "Move! Move! Faster!"

Commando: A prison work group.

Jewish women pulling hopper cars of quarried stone in the Plaszow Concentration Camp in Poland. During World War II, the Nazis forced millions of people into concentration camps and used the captives as slaves.

Eight kilometers: About five miles.

Twenty-five to thirty cubic meters: About thirty-tree to thirty-nine cubic yards.

had to walk **eight kilometers** to our job, and, of course, each evening, eight kilometers back to the camp. Our worn-out shoes alone would have made this march painful, but our exhaustion made it torturous. The roadbed for this section of the future railroad ran across open fields. Each one of us was assigned a definite work quota. Each day, working as a team of two, we were required to load a certain number of tip trucks with **twenty-five to thirty cubic meters** of earth. This demand was unreasonable, for the ground was so hard and stony that first we had to break it with a pick. We were digging our own graves in the German earth! I could still swing my pick fairly well, buy many of my friends were noticeably weakening. What would happen to them if we should be forced to spend another winter here? We were so famished that once again our hunger became an obsession. It was absolutely essential to relax our pace, but we were watched too closely. Strange as it may seem, some worked rapidly just to make trouble for others. At Laura, as well as here, I had observed that some prisoners—poor intimidated fellows, robots of the System—killed themselves with work when they could have

Slavery in the Belgian Congo

In the 1880s, it seemed that slavery was finished. In 1886, the institution came to an end in Cuba, and Brazil followed suit two years later. Yet that same decade saw the rebirth of slavery in the Congo, a huge region in southern central Africa formed by the basin of the Congo River. Promising to protect the people of the Congo from Arab slavers, King Leopold of Belgium in 1885 assumed control over the vast country, which he proceeded to turn into his personal colony.

Over the next twenty-three years, Leopold ruled the absurdly named "Congo Free State" with almost unimaginable cruelty. The Belgian Congo, an area seventy-five times as large as Belgium itself, was rich in natural resources and treasures, which Leopold exploited by using slave laborers. His overseers set impossibly high quotas for workers, and when the latter failed to meet them, would cut off their hands.

The Belgians also kidnaped women and children, and in the latter days of Leopold's rule, resorted to wholesale slaughter of populations who failed to produce. In the end, they killed about half the Congo's population of 20,000,000 before Leopold was forced to turn over control of the colony to the Belgian government in 1908. Leopold himself never set foot in the Congo.

The Belgian Congo was the last clear-cut example of white Europeans enslaving black Africans, as in the early modern era. In its almost limitless brutality, however, the Congo experience compared to the crimes of the twentieth century. Thus in a sense it might be considered a bridge between one era of slavery and another.

*limited their output. We marked them well, for by increasing production norms, they involuntarily became our enemies. They worked to their own **detriment**, and most of them did not last long.*

*Since we were fortunate enough to work under a reasonable foreman, I did not try to transfer to another commando. Admittedly, in spite of ourselves, our team worked decidedly harder than the others, but thereby we gained some small advantages. The **SS** supervisor distributed tobacco to us as often as an **unprecedented** three times a week. I did not smoke, but tobacco was a valuable currency; with two or three cigarettes, I could buy a liter of soup. Perhaps it is surprising that soup was for sale in the camp. However, there was nothing we could do about the **black market**; we were governed by the law of our environment. The German prisoners, who distributed the soup, set aside several containers for a company of **profiteers**,*

Late Modern Slavery (1900–Present): Aimé Bonifas

Detriment: Harm.

SS: Abbreviation of *Schutzstaffel,* or "protective unit" in German. The SS were elite troops who did much of the Nazis' killing.

Unprecedented: Something of which there is no earlier example.

Black market: The illegal buying and selling of goods.

Profiteers: People who make an unreasonable profit by taking advantage of shortages to charge extremely high prices.

Allied soldiers crawling past
log fortifications on the
beach of Normandy during
D-Day on June 6, 1944. D-
Day was a turning point in
World War II and led to the
liberation of countless
prisoners from Nazi
concentration camps.
*Reproduced by permission of
Corbis Corporation (Bellevue).*

the **Slavic** dishwashers, who ate what they wanted and black-mar-
keted the rest.

What happened next...

    In all, Bonifas was confined at five camps, as signified
by chapter titles in *Prisoner 20-801:* "Compiégne, Detention
Camp"; "Buchenwald, the Gates of Hell"; "Laura, Extermination Camp"; "Mackenrode, Forced Labor Camp"; "Osterha-
gen, Disciplinary Camp."

    The war raged on, with Germany losing more and
more territory. The Nazis had done little to win the sympathy
of conquered peoples, who aided the Allies (United States,

Slavic: A term that
encompasses a number of
Eastern European national
groups such as Russians,
Poles, and Czechs.

Britain, and the Soviet Union) in driving the Germans back. One reason for Hitler's eventual defeat was his obsession with killing Jews. At a time when his troops desperately needed shipments of munitions and other goods, he ordered the deployment of railroads to transport Jewish prisoners to extermination camps instead of transporting supplies to the troops.

Once American, British, and other Allied troops invaded Europe in June 1944, the Nazi cause was finished. With the Allies descending on his capital at Berlin, Hitler committed suicide on April 30, 1945, and Germany surrendered a week later. Allied troops liberated countless prisoners in extermination and death camps; unfortunately, prisoners in Eastern Europe, where the Soviets assumed control, were simply moved from a Nazi slave-labor camp to a Soviet one.

Fortunately for Bonifas, he was in the western part of Europe, dominated by the British, Americans, and other democratic nations. After the war, he studied for the ministry and became a pastor. He published *Prisoner 20-801* in French in 1946, and a Spanish edition followed in 1949. Not one but four German editions followed and the book was translated into English in 1983. During the 1980s and 1990s, Bonifas wrote and published several books attacking Holocaust denial, which is the effort by Nazi sympathizers to "prove" that the Holocaust never happened.

Did you know...

- Ironically, the Nazis won power not by overthrowing the government, as was typical of most totalitarian regimes, but by winning an election.

- The term "concentration camp" refers to the fact that a large population is concentrated within the camp.

- The first concentration camps were used not by the Nazis or Soviets, but by the British, who interned captured South African soldiers in such camps during the Boer War (1899–1902).

For more information

Books

Bonifas, Aimé. *Prisoner 20-801: A French National in the Nazi Labor Camps.*

Translated by Claude R. Foster Jr., and Mildred M. Van Sice from the 4th French Edition, with a foreword by Franklin H. Littell. Carbondale: Southern Illinois University Press, 1987.

Sources

Books

Green, Robert. *Dictators of the Modern World.* San Diego: Lucent Books, 2000.

Langley, Andrew. *100 Greatest Tyrants.* Danbury, Conn.: Grolier Educational, 1997.

Wepman, Dennis. *Germany under Hitler.* New York: F. Watts, 1997.

Whittock, Martyn J. *Hitler and National Socialism.* Des Plaines, Ill.: Rigby Interactive Library, 1996.

Other

Freedom, Democide, War. http://www2.hawaii.edu/~rummel/ (Accessed on May 12, 2000).

Yun Turi

Excerpt from **True Stories of the Korean Comfort Women**
Published in *True Stories of the Korean Comfort Women*, 1995
Edited by Keith Howard

G ermany and Japan fought on the same side during World
War II (1939–45), an alliance known as the Axis nations.
They did little to coordinate their efforts, but their leaders
shared a desire to rule the world and a brutal disregard of
human rights. Japan, a nation lacking in natural resources,
wanted to conquer eastern Asia and the Pacific islands, and it
very nearly succeeded in doing so.

In 1931, ten years before Japanese planes launched a
surprise attack on Pearl Harbor, Hawaii, which brought the
United States into World War II against Japan and Germany,
Japan annexed Manchuria in northern China. During the
1930s, the Japanese tightened their grip on China, and by
1941, they were prepared to extend their rule over much of
the region. On December 7, the same day as the Pearl Harbor
attack, Japan launched attacks in several other areas, including the Philippines. Japan did not attack Korea, however, simply because it had already controlled that country since 1910.

Conquered nations unwillingly supplied Japan with
both natural resources and human resources, including both
regular slave labor and a type of sex slave known in Japan as

> There was no single
> happy moment during
> my life as a comfort
> woman.

The Bridge on the River Kwai

In addition to "comfort women," Japan adopted more well-known forms of slavery during World War II, including the use of prisoners of war (POWs) to build bridges and other large public projects. This experience is brilliantly portrayed in the film *The Bridge on the River Kwai* (1957), a fictional account of British soldiers forced by the Japanese to build a rail bridge through a jungle in Burma. The film won numerous Academy Awards, including Best Picture, Best Director (David Lean), and Best Actor (Alec Guinness). The storyline of *The Bridge on the River Kwai* illustrates the means by which slaves and prisoners often came to identify with their captors.

"comfort women." This term is a euphemism, or an attempt to soften the meaning of something by giving it a nice-sounding name. No mere words, however, can soften the reality of forced prostitution (the practice of engaging in sex acts for hire), a hideous form of slavery and personal violation that these women had to endure.

From the early 1930s to the end of World War II in 1945, as many as 200,000 women between the ages of eleven and thirty-two were forced to attend to the sexual desires of Japanese servicemen, often several dozen men a day. The majority of "comfort women," like Yun Turi in the passage below, came from Korea; but plenty more of these women were from the Philippines, China, and other nations. They contracted sexually transmitted diseases, underwent unwanted pregnancies and dangerous abortions, and suffered enormous shame.

Things to remember while reading

- Yun Turi served in a "comfort house" in Pusan, a large city on the Sea of Japan in southeastern Korea. The coast of Japan was only about two hundred miles away, making Pusan a convenient location for Japanese servicemen.

- In using the expression "venereal disease," Yun Turi harkened back to another era. Prior to the appearance of AIDS (Acquired Immunodeficiency Syndrome) in the early 1980s, venereal diseases such as syphilis and gonorrhea were the most feared variety of sexually transmitted disease.

- From Yun Turi's reference to "that fateful day," it is easy enough to guess that she was kidnaped and forced to serve as a prostitute. As for her weeping when she heard that her mother was selling herbs, this was because she realized how vulnerable her mother and younger siblings were without her. Their father was dead, and Yun Turi had been the principal breadwinner for the family; now her mother was reduced to selling herbs, a grave dishonor in Yun Turi's mind.

True Stories of the Korean Comfort Women

I served, on average, 30 to 40 men daily. They were mostly sailors and soldiers posted to Pusan. When a ship came into harbor, many sailors visited us. At weekends, many more would come than on weekdays. When I had to serve many men, I would go out of my mind. The men would enter my room one after another, and it was impossible to count them. After I had served a soldier, I went downstairs to wash myself with water mixed with **creosol**. *Then I returned to serve the next man. To lessen the number I served even by one, I insisted on washing each time and tried to prolong the time I took cleaning up after each. The soldiers were supposed to use condoms, but many tried to avoid them. Many of them were nasty....*

Some soldiers were kind. Yosimura came to see me often, and he took pity on my **plight** *and did not try to sleep with me. He was a soldier. He took my photograph and said he wanted to marry me once the war ended. He said that he would take me to Japan after his country won the war. I tearfully pleaded with him to help me leave the place, but he replied that he lacked any real power. He couldn't do anything because I was there on the orders of his superiors. He sometimes gave me sweets or money. After Japan lost the war, he went back to Japan alone. There was another man who often visited me. He said he had Korean parents, but that he had been born in Japan and was now a sailor in the* **Imperial Forces** *His ship came to Pusan once a month, and he visited me each time. Once I went to the harbor with him to see his ship. He, together with several other officers, got permission to take us out and bring us back. That was the only time I left the station. Others went out occasionally with soldiers for short* **liaisons** *but, in principle, we were not allowed out.*

I never got pregnant at the station, but two others did. One died while having an abortion. The other grew quite large with the baby, and tried to commit suicide by hanging herself from a banister. But

Creosol: An oily, aromatic substance obtained from wood tar and often used to kill germs.

Plight: Unfortunate situation.

Imperial Forces: The Japanese military, or in this case the Japanese navy.

Liaisons: Sexual encounters.

WPA Slave Narratives

During the 1930s, slavery was taking different forms such as the Japanese "comfort women" system and the labor camps of Soviet Russia. At the same time, victims of earlier forms of slavery, such as the kind practiced in the American South in the nineteenth century, were dying off—not from the effects of slave labor, but from old age.

Between 1936 to 1938, the Works Progress Administration (WPA), a unit of the federal government under the administration of President Franklin D. Roosevelt, interviewed more than 2,300 former slaves in the American South. By then, more than seventy years had passed since the end of slavery in the United States, and the people interviewed by the WPA had experienced slavery only as small children. WPA researchers knew that if they wanted to get the stories of these former slaves down on paper, they had to act quickly.

For more about the WPA slave narratives, visit a Web site created by the University of Virginia: http://xroads.virginia.edu/~HYPER/wpa/wphahome.html (accessed on May 12, 2000).

she was discovered by a soldier and taken away. I don't know were she ended up. Nobody had any children at the station. When we had our monthly periods we were given gauze *in lieu of* sanitary towels, which we used whenever we weren't serving the soldiers. But we were made to serve soldiers even while menstruating, so we had no time to keep the towels in place. I can't describe how dirty and miserable the whole thing was. When we had to continue having sex while menstruating, we rolled the gauze up and inserted it deep into our wombs. Once I couldn't get it out again, and became very worried. In the end I had to go to hospital to have it removed.

The hospital was right next to the comfort station. It had a male doctor and a nurse who gave us check-ups for *venereal disease* once a month. The doctor looked into our insides, inserting his fingers. Anyone infected with *gonorrhea* was given the "No. 606" injection. This hurt your arm so much that you felt it would drop off your body. I was infected once. I went to the hospital for injections and took a lot of medicine. Even after I left the station, the infection would flare up whenever I became weak.

Many officers stayed the night. When they stayed over, in what was *euphemistically* described as "sleeping the long night," I would leave the bedroom and stand out in the hall even in the cold winter to reduce the hours I had to spend with them a little. Once a week, when there were no officers staying overnight, I was able to sleep comfortably. Those who stayed left at five the next morning. Then we could sleep better, but we had to be up at 7.30 a.m. We had to gather in the yard, sing the Japanese anthem, and recite the Oath of Imperial Subjects. Only then did we get breakfast between 8.00 and 9.00 o'clock. We had a break for an hour and then the soldiers began to arrive. The largest number would arrive at between 3.00 and 4.00 p.m. We were allowed 30 minutes for meals, during which time we weren't forced to serve soldiers. Of the women in the station, I still remember Yun Yongja, who had the Japanese name Yamamoto Eiko, Umeko and Sunja.

A fortnight after my arrival, I tried to escape. Sunja said she knew the area around Yongdo, so we tried to run away together. I was the one who suggested it. To get past the two guards, we pretended to be nice to them and offered them cigarettes. We asked if we could go out for some fresh air, but they wouldn't allow it, so we offered them drinks, after which they sat down in the hall and began to doze. We sneaked out, pretending we were off to the toilet, and then ran. But the road outside the station was longer than we had thought, and we were caught before we had got more than a few steps. After that I was hit hard three times on my hip with a gun, and I fell on my belly with blood pouring from my mouth. The wound on my hip left a big bruise and became infected, giving me an accompanying high fever. I was unable to lie on my back, but even in that state I had to keep on serving soldiers. The wound **festered** and became rotten. Only then did the soldiers take me to the hospital to have the rotten part cut out. I was allowed to take a break for three days. Then, even though it was still impossible for me to lie on my back, the soldiers started to visit me again. This was the hardest time of my confinement. It was too painful to serve soldiers when I couldn't even lie on my back. All the women harbored thoughts of running away, but after they saw me beaten and suffering, they gave up. Nobody attempted to flee anymore.

There was no single happy moment during my life as a comfort woman. When the soldiers didn't visit us and we were left on our own, we talked of our homes and wept. When the Japanese soldiers did visit, they often lined us up and took photographs. I would sing my two favorite songs, Arirang and To My Mother. When I missed my mother, I sang the latter song and cried. We had to sing anything in Korean in secret, since if we were caught we would be severely reprimanded. I never wrote to my family nor received a letter from them. No correspondence and no visits were allowed. But I once heard news. I was looking out of the window when I saw a peddler from my neighborhood. I asked him about my mother, and he told me she was selling herbs. I wept a lot when I heard this.

I now know that, when I didn't return home that fateful day, my mother and sister had gone round trying to find me. My sister even

Venereal disease: Sexually transmitted diseases.

Gonorrhea: A sexually transmitted disease.

Euphemistically: An euphemism is a gentler expression used in place of something more offensive—but perhaps more accurate.

A fortnight: Two weeks.

Festered: Generated pus.

came to the comfort station in case I had been taken there. Since the building had once been a guest-house it was on the street and we could see passers-by from the windows. They came by again on a day when no soldiers were visiting, and I saw them while I was looking out of the window. I rushed down to greet them. My mother saw me and tried to take me back, but the soldiers pushed them both away, and we were parted without being able to say a single word to each other. After that my mother was so upset she became ill. There was a sign-board and guards, so they must have realized I had become a comfort woman. There was also a second comfort station in Pusan, in Taesin ward. I hear that there were about 40 to 50 women in that place.

What happened next...

Japan surrendered to the Allies (the United States, Britain, and the Soviet Union) on September 2, 1945. Korea and other countries were liberated, and the "comfort women" were freed to return to their homes. Determined to provide for her family and embarrassed that she had no money, Yun Turi got a job as a waitress at a restaurant near the "comfort station." She worked for a year and saved her money before going home to her mother, her younger sister, and brothers.

Yun Turi recalled her return: "My mother was out selling vegetables at a market, and my younger sister greeted me with tears in her eyes. At 6.00 in the evening my mother, haggard and with a faded dark complexion, came home. To see her like that broke my heart. She wept. I wept. She wept, saying that she had thought she would never see me again. The following morning, she was ready to go out to sell her vegetables, but I stopped her. With the money I had, we first bought rice. Later, I worked and earned sufficient money to bring up my brothers and sister."

Many of the comfort women believed they were somehow responsible for what had happened to them. In their shame, these women feared, in some cases correctly, that their families would not take them back, or would view them as collaborators with the Japanese. Not every homecoming was as positive as Yun Turi's.

Shame also kept the former "comfort women" silent for nearly fifty years. Yet in the 1990s, they began to speak out. Groups of former victims petitioned the Japanese government for financial compensation and apologies. Though they received an apology from Prime Minister Keizo Obuchi in October 1998, it was small compensation for the horrors they had suffered. However, the story was not over: as people in the United States and other Western countries became more aware that the "comfort women" had existed, their cause began to gain more support.

Former Korean comfort women sitting outside the gate of parliament in Tokyo protesting for an apology for the injustices they faced at the hands of the Japanese government during World War II.
Reproduced by permission of AP/Wide World Photos, Inc.

Did you know...
- A geisha is a Japanese woman trained to provide entertainment to men. Unlike comfort women geishas are not prostitutes, but are highly sophisticated women admired for their ability to offer stimulating conversation.

- After World War II, Korea was divided into two nations: North Korea, with a communist government supported by the Soviet Union and later China, and South Korea, whose government the United States supported. Under the leadership of dictator Kim Il-Sung (1912–1994) and his son and successor, Kim Jong-Il, North Korea became one of the most brutally repressive countries on Earth, one that made extensive use of slave labor.

- Until the early twentieth century, some upper-class Chinese women were subjected to a custom called foot-binding. Because Chinese men considered tiny feet on a woman attractive, the tiny feet of the little girls would be bound tightly starting in infancy, thus stunting their growth. As a result, women whose feet had been bound were hardly able to walk.

For more information

Books

Howard, Keith, ed. *True Stories of the Korean Comfort Women: Testimonies Compiled by the Korean Council for Women Drafted for Military Sexual Slavery by Japan and the Research Association on the Women Drafted for Military Sexual Slavery by Japan, and Translated by Young Joo Lee*. London: Cassell, 1995.

Sources

Books

Schmidt, David A. *Ianfu, the Comfort Women of the Imperial Army of the Pacific War: Broken Silence*. Lewiston, NY: Edwin Mellen Press, 2000.

Periodicals

Coday, Dennis J. "'I Cannot Die Without an Apology': Korean Women Forced into Sexual Slavery Await Words That Will Ease Torment." *National Catholic Reporter,* October 23, 1998, p. 14.

McCormack, Gavan. "Japan's Uncomfortable Past." *History Today,* May 1998, p. 5.

"War Memories." *The Economist* (U.S.), August 15, 1998, p. 31.

Other

Comfort Women. http://www.hk.co.kr/event/jeonshin/e_homepage.htm (Accessed on May 12, 2000).

American Federation of Labor

"Free Labor vs. Slave Labor: Irrepressible Conflict"

Published in *Slave Labor in Russia: The Case Presented by the American Federation of Labor to the United Nations*, 1949

At the beginning of World War II (1939–45), the Soviet Union (a former country of eastern Europe and northern Asia that united Russia and various other soviet republics) under Joseph Stalin (1879–1953) had been allied with Nazi Germany; however, the German invasion of the Soviet Union in 1941 had ended this alliance. As a result, the Soviet Union joined forces with Great Britain and the United States against Nazi Germany. Even before the war ended in 1945, this alliance was falling apart, largely because of different ways they treated human life: America and Britain were, for all their faults, countries with a high value for freedom and human life, whereas Stalin's regime was built on slave labor, repression, and death.

By 1947, when the American Federation of Labor (AFL) published a statement in its *International Free Trade Union News* denouncing Soviet slave-labor practices, the wartime alliance was in shreds. The United States and Soviet Union had entered into an undeclared conflict, known as the Cold War, which would continue until the fall of Soviet Communism (a system of government in which the state plans

> To those who excuse the Soviet methods on the ground that such practices serve the aims of socialism, the reply can only be that the founders of the socialist doctrine proclaimed it as a path for workers' liberation, and not their enslavement.

and controls the economy and a single, often authoritarian state) in the late 1980s and early 1990s. During this time, American opinion about the Soviet system was divided, with many Americans professing admiration for the Soviets' stated aims of social and economic equality, even if they did not admire their methods.

This division was particularly strong within the U.S. labor movement. Labor unions are organizations of workers that use their large numbers and political power to obtain higher wages, shorter hours, and other concessions. During the late nineteenth and early twentieth centuries, the unions were often on the same side as communist and socialist groups in their opposition to factory owners and management. (Socialism is a social system in which the means of producing and distributing goods are owned collectively and political power is exercised by the whole community.) However, as the industrial systems of the Western world modified and adapted to the labor unions, unionists and political radicals went their separate ways.

Nonetheless, the admiration of many in the labor movement for the stated aims of communism blinded many to the crimes committed by Stalin and others. Hence the AFL's statement: "To those who excuse the Soviet methods on the ground that such practices serve the aims of socialism, the reply can only be that the founders of the socialist doctrine proclaimed it as a path for workers' liberation, and not their enslavement. In discussing the totalitarian system of slavery now represented by the Soviet Union, the problem of socialism as such, does not enter."

Much of the Soviet system's appeal to workers and others in the West was its use of powerful words, which contrasted sharply with reality. The AFL addressed this issue by stating, "In spite of the high-sounding declarations of the Soviet Constitution, the Russian political police still retains the power, conferred upon it by a decree of 1934, to send anyone to a concentration camp without a trial."

The first Five-Year Plan was another example of the difference between image and reality in Stalin's regime. Instituted in 1928 by Stalin's regime, the plan was an effort to jump-start Soviet agriculture and industry by setting goals and then pushing to achieve them. In fact, as the AFL noted,

The Nightmare of Stalinism

Virtually every American knows about their nation's history of slavery, or about the Nazi's extermination of the Jews during the Holocaust. Yet perhaps only one in ten has heard about the horrors associated with the rule of Joseph Stalin in the Soviet Union, despite the fact that Stalin's crimes impacted more people than both American slavery and the Holocaust. From the time he took power in the late 1920s until his death in 1953, Stalin either directly or indirectly caused the deaths of tens of millions of people.

Though the purges referred to by the AFL were devastating, they were mainly directed at political opponents or enemies of the state, and thus involved a relatively small number of people. Much worse was the death toll associated with Stalin's Five-Year plans and the collectivization of agriculture. Both of these massive Soviet efforts were implemented in the late 1920s; both were attempts to push the Soviet economy forward rapidly. Each also used huge slave-labor brigades made up of ordinary citizens.

Under collectivization, millions of peasants were forcibly removed from their homes and herded onto giant agricultural facilities called collective farms. Many died in transport, or were killed, and many more died because they refused to work. In some cases, peasants burned their crops rather than turn them over to Stalin; this resulted in man-made famines. The peasants who did go to work on the collective farms became virtual slaves, yet their situation was preferable to that of the prisoners forced to work in mines or on giant construction projects.

Eventually Stalin established a network of slave-labor camps, called the *gulag.* Later, the Russian writer Aleksandr Solzhenitsyn (1918–), a former slave laborer in the camps, gave this network a memorable name when he exposed the camp system in *The Gulag Archipelago* (1973). An archipelago is a group of islands, and indeed the prisons were like a series of islands dotting the frozen northern section of Russia. By the time Solzhenitsyn published his book, Stalin was long dead, and many of the labor camps had been closed. However, the Soviet Union continued to make use of "corrective labor," though on a smaller scale.

the plan involved huge amounts of slave labor; although Stalin announced in 1933 that the goals had all been exceeded— and in less time than anticipated—this is highly unlikely. In any case, the cost in human lives was so high that no government with a respect for human rights would pursue such a plan even if it *did* work.

The AFL aimed to show by its statement that, although Nazism (the ideology and practice of the Nazis, especially the policy of racist nationalism, national expansion, and state control of the economy) had recently been destroyed, another form of totalitarianism, one on which Hitler had modeled aspects of his Nazi state, continued to flourish in the Soviet Union. As a leading representative of free labor, the AFL declared its strong opposition to Soviet use of slave labor, noting that the use of slave labor anywhere was an offense to free labor everywhere.

Things to remember while reading

- The statement by the AFL refers extensively to the history and politics of the mid-twentieth century, for instance, the Nazi-Soviet pact of August 1939. This was an agreement between Germany and the Soviet Union that neither would attack the other, and it made possible Hitler's invasion of Poland, the event that initiated World War II on September 1, 1939. Stalin took advantage of the pact to acquire parts of Poland, as well as Latvia, Lithuania, and Estonia. On June 22, 1941, Hitler broke the pact by invading the Soviet Union.

- In addition, the AFL statement refers to a new series of purges in the Soviet Union. During the purges of the 1930s, Stalin had arranged for the arrest and execution of many thousands of people, almost always on false charges, or no charges at all. During the war with Nazi Germany, however, he needed the Soviet people's help, and therefore discontinued the purges and other attacks on the population. As soon as the war ended, though, Stalin launched a new series of purges, particularly against people he accused of helping the Nazis.

- Established in 1922, the Soviet Union included both "republics," the largest of which was Russia, and tiny "autonomous" (independent) republics. In fact there was nothing autonomous about these, as the AFL's statement—"several autonomous republics were abolished and their entire populations deported"—makes clear.

- The AFL referred to Yugoslavia, Bulgaria, and Poland as "satellite states of the Soviet Union." In fact Yugoslavia

later broke away from Soviet influence and charted a separate course for itself, as did Albania and Romania, two other communist nations in Eastern Europe. However, the Soviet Union retained a high degree of control over Poland, East Germany, Czechoslovakia, Hungary, and Bulgaria. The Sudeten districts of Czechoslovakia comprised an area with a heavy German population. In 1938 Hitler had used the concentration of Germans there as an excuse to take over the region.

Russian slave laborers building the "Stalin Canal" under Joseph Stalin's Five-Year Plan.
Reproduced by permission of Archive Photos, Inc.

"Free Labor vs. Slave Labor: Irrepressible Conflict"

About a quarter of a century ago it seemed as if the complete extinction of the last remnants of slavery throughout the world might not be far off. Slavery had been outlawed by international **conventions** *and its abolition in those backward countries where it still existed was, apparently, only a question of time.*

However, the rise of **totalitarianism** *brought about a complete reversal of this historical trend. During the last 20 years the world has witnessed the reintroduction of slavery on a gigantic scale. The widespread use of forced labor by the modern dictatorships and those under their influence is, indeed, nothing but a reappearance of slavery under a different name. This* **reversion to servitude**—*and that is what it is, in the literal sense of the word*—*is one of the principal characteristics of modern totalitarianism and totalitarian tendencies.*

The process of creating huge forced labor armies began in Russia under the first Five-Year Plan. Since that time, slave labor has become a regular and integral factor of the Russian economy as it has developed under subsequent Five-Year Plans. A net of so-called corrective labor camps has been gradually extended all over the Soviet Union. Various estimates of the number of the inmates of these camps have been made, but the figure of 10,000,000—not including prisoners of war and other deported non-Soviet citizens—seems to be not exaggerated.

When Hitler seized power in Germany, he immediately followed the Soviet example by creating **concentration camps** *for political opponents and any other persons whom the Nazi regime considered harmful; and when the Nazis overran Europe they created an immense reservoir of forced labor by* **deporting** *millions of workers to Germany.*

But the defeat and destruction of the Nazi dictatorship has failed to ring the **knell** *for the system of modern slavery which had been introduced by totalitarianism. The situation in Russia remains unchanged. In spite of the high-sounding declarations of the Soviet* **Constitution***, the Russian political police still retains the power, conferred upon it by a decree of 1934, to send anyone to a concentra-*

Conventions: Agreements.

Totalitarianism: Any of several political systems, most notably communism, fascism, and Nazism, in which the government exercises total control over the populace.

Reversion to servitude: Return to slavery.

Concentration camps: Large prisons in which political prisoners, or prisoners of war (POWs), are detained.

Deporting: Forcibly removing.

Knell: The sound of a bell ringing slowly, as at a funeral; an indication of the end of something.

Constitution: A set of written laws governing a nation.

tion camp without a trial. The provision of this decree that the political police may not impose terms in concentration camps for longer than five years is virtually meaningless, since the practice is to impose additional terms after the expiration of the first. There is no indication that the Soviet government has thought of rewarding the sufferings and sacrifices of the peoples of the Soviet Union during the war by abolishing or reducing the number of concentration camps, or by liberating any appreciable portion of their gigantic forced labor army. On the contrary, we have been informed that as a collective punishment for the **collaborationism** of some, several autonomous republics were abolished and their entire populations deported.

The new **purges** sweeping all sections of Soviet public and economic life indicate that the activities of the Soviet political police, aimed at assuring a constant supply of forced labor, are as ruthless as ever.

Not only has the forced labor situation failed to improve inside the borders of the Soviet Union, but the Soviet government has extended its methods far beyond its own frontiers. Reports from Yugoslavia, Bulgaria and Poland prove that the Russian system of concentration camps and forced labor has been fully adopted by the **satellite states** of the Soviet Union. In addition, the Soviet government has continued the practice which it inaugurated in 1939 and 1940 when, during its pact with Hitler, it occupied the Eastern provinces of Poland and the Baltic states and deported over 1,000,000 Poles and a considerable number of Lithuanians, **Letts** and Estonians to remote parts of the Soviet Union. Recently, the deportation of German workers from the Soviet zone of occupation was resumed on a large scale. The mass expulsions of the German population from their homes in the Sudeten districts of Czechoslovakia and in the Eastern provinces of Germany are intimately connected with the system of totalitarian slavery.

Such treatment of millions of people, driven from their homes after being stripped of all their possessions, is conceivable only in a political and moral climate saturated and infected by the totalitarian practice of slave-raiding—a practice in which, unfortunately, other powers have so far diplomatically **acquiesced**.

The question of German war prisoners must also be considered from this point of view. Eighteen months have passed since the **cessation** of hostilities in Europe, but there are still more than 3,000,000 German war prisoners in Russia (to say nothing of the still uncounted number of Japanese), about 600,000 in France and

Collaborationism: A policy of aiding the enemies of one's own nation.

Purges: Massive efforts by Stalin's government to find and kill supposed enemies of the state.

Satellite states: Countries politically, militarily, and economically dominated by a larger country.

Letts: Latvians.

Acquiesced: Submitted or complied.

Cessation: Conclusion.

*360,000 in England. These are being used for forced labor. In this particular instance, it is done under the **guise** of collecting **reparations**. However, **servitude is prejudicial to free labor** and to human liberty in general, regardless of the pretext under which it is practiced. It is particularly **deplorable** that democratic nations should make use of the forced labor of war prisoners, and thereby help to fortify the totalitarian system of outright slavery as it exists in the Soviet Union.*

*Free labor has always opposed slave labor in any form or under any pretext. Slave labor anywhere in the world adversely affects the standards of free labor everywhere. Moreover, each highly centralized political system based on slavery **engenders** aggressive policies, since it tends to enslave new populations in order to satisfy its need for an additional supply of forced labor. Furthermore, such a system tends to resort to conquest as a means of acquiring sources of wealth which it cannot create fast enough because of the notoriously low productivity of slave labor.*

*There is really an "irrepressible conflict" between free labor and every system of forced labor. To those who excuse the Soviet methods on the ground that such practices serve the aims of **socialism**, the reply can only be that the founders of the socialist doctrine proclaimed it as a path for workers' liberation, and not their enslavement. In discussing the totalitarian system of slavery now represented by the Soviet Union, **the problem of socialism as such, does not enter**. In this case the question is simply one of free labor versus slave labor.*

The A. F. of L. has condemned all forms of forced labor and servitude. The A. F. of L., through its Bill of Rights, appeals to all forces of free labor throughout the world to support it in this crucial struggle.

Guise: False appearance.

Reparations: Payment from an individual, group, or nation for harm previously caused.

Servitude is prejudicial to free labor: In other words, the use of slave labor is harmful to the aims and purposes of free labor.

Deplorable: Worthy of scorn or objection.

Engenders: To give rise to.

Socialism: A highly modified form of communism, in which much greater individual freedom and ownership are allowed; *socialism* was often used as a euphemism—a deceptively gentle-sounding term—for Soviet Communism.

The problem of socialism as such, does not enter: In other words, one does not have to oppose the idea of socialism in order to oppose Soviet practices.

What happened next...

The AFL's statement against Soviet slave labor appeared in the January 1947 issue of *International Free Trade Union News*, a publication of the Free Trade Union of the American Federation of Labor. Two years later, the AFL included the editorial in documents it presented to the United

THE RED MILL

SLAVE LABOR

RUSSIAN ECONOMY

From the daily newspaper THE MANCHESTER MORNING UNION,
Manchester, New Hampshire, U.S.A.

A political cartoon illustrating how the Russian economy was built on slave labor.
Courtesy of The Library of Congress.

Nations (UN) as part of an effort to urge UN condemnation of Soviet slave-labor practices.

The UN had been founded at the end of World War II with the aim of providing an international organization to ensure peace and justice around the world. However, the Cold War prevented it from becoming a workable body, because the Soviet Union's influence in the UN gave it full

The American Federation of Labor

A union is an organization of workers that uses its large numbers and political power to obtain concessions from management, such as higher wages and shorter hours. Groups of unions, representing specific trades such as transportation workers or bricklayers, often come together in even larger groups called union federations. The American Federation of Labor or AFL, sometimes referred to as the A. F. of L., was the largest and most enduring union federation in American history.

Founded in 1886, the AFL became a powerful force under the leadership of Samuel Gompers (1850–1924), who served as its president for thirty-seven years. It had 1,000,000 members in 1902, a number that doubled by World War I (1914–18), and doubled again to 4,000,000 by 1920. However, under the leadership of William Green, who served from 1924 to 1952, the AFL encountered a number of new challenges brought on in part by the economic hardships associated with the Great Depression (1929–41).

Many groups within the federation were critical of the manner in which the AFL responded to these challenges, and in 1938 several unions broke away to form the Congress of Industrial Organizations (CIO). Seventeen years later, the two organizations merged to form the AFL-CIO. At the end of the twentieth century, the AFL-CIO represented about 14,000,000 of the estimated 20,000,000 U.S. union members.

power to cancel out any initiatives by the United States or other democratic nations. For that reason, the AFL's message had little direct impact in the short run.

In the years that followed, the Cold War escalated while Stalin's death brought to light some (but not nearly all) of his crimes. Meanwhile the AFL merged with the CIO (Congress of Industrial Organizations) in 1955 to form the AFL-CIO. This new organization increasingly concentrated on matters of more direct concern to U.S. workers than the slave-labor practices of the Soviet Union.

The end of Soviet Communism in 1991 led to the full disclosure of crimes by Stalin and other Soviet leaders. Without Soviet influence opposing it at every turn, the UN became a more effective organization. In the 1990s, it took more active efforts in opposition to slavery worldwide.

Did you know...

- In *Modern Times* (1983), author Paul Johnson reported that in the confusion created by Stalin's massive arrests and deportations, one Soviet citizen was arrested, sentenced to die, pardoned, then sent to a labor camp, only be released and awarded a medal—all within eighteen months. He never knew what crime he supposedly had committed in the first place.

- The Soviet Union, also called the U.S.S.R. or Union of Soviet Socialist Republics, comprised fifteen "republics." In terms of both geography and population, Russia was much larger than the other fourteen combined. After the breakup of the Soviet Union in 1991, these republics became independent countries.

- During the Great Depression of the 1930s, some Americans defected to the Soviet Union, that is, they gave up their U.S. citizenship, planning never to return. Many of these people ended up in prison camps, and some later managed to escape and return to America.

For more information

Books

American Federation of Labor. *Slave Labor in Russia: The Case Presented by the American Federation of Labor to the United Nations*. Washington, D.C.: American Federation of Labor, 1949.

Sources

Books

Herling, Albert Konrad. *The Soviet Slave Empire*. New York: W. Funk, 1951.

Kallen, Stuart A. *The Stalin Era: 1925–1953*. Edited by Rosemary Wallner. Edina, Minn.: Abdo & Daughters, 1992.

Matthews, John R. *The Rise and Fall of the Soviet Union*. San Diego: Lucent Books, 2000.

Otfinoski, Steven. *Joseph Stalin: Russia's Last Czar*. Brookfield, Conn.: Millbrook Press, 1993.

The Khmer Rouge were battle-hardened guerrilla warriors who had long fought government forces in the jungles of Cambodia. Many were illiterate, and quite a few were young. It might be said that they were teenagers with guns. Their guidance came from an elite group of Cambodian scholars who had studied in Paris. These scholars, sometimes referred to as *Angka Loeu,* admired the radical Communism applied by Mao Zedong (1893–1976) in China, and determined that Cambodia needed to undergo a purifying process. All foreign influences would have to be removed, and the people would need to return to the land and work the soil by ancient methods.

This was a recipe for a slave-labor system of unparalleled brutality. Following their victory on April 17, 1975, Khmer Rouge tanks rolled into the capital city, Phnom Penh (NAHM PEN) and forced Cambodians into the countryside. Anyone who asked questions was shot, as was anyone suspected of corruption in any form—including people who wore eyeglasses, which was seen a sign that they were educated, sophisticated, and therefore, dangerous.

The survivors were herded into the countryside and put to work on rice farms, where they labored for incredibly long hours, without days off, and did not receive adequate nutrition. In the rare hours when they were not working, the people were forced to undergo "re-education" classes, in which they were encouraged to report on suspicious activities of their neighbors.

It was all part of the remaking of Cambodia, which the Khmer Rouge renamed as Kampuchea. The year 1975 also had a new name: "Year Zero," the beginning of a new era. François Ponchaud, a Roman Catholic priest who lived for many years in Cambodia, chose the phrase as the title for his book exposing the crimes of the Khmer Rouge. Ponchaud had been forced to leave, along with all other foreigners, in 1975, and obtained most of the material for the book by interviewing Cambodian refugees.

Things to remember while reading

- The following passage includes extensive references (some of which have been removed) to Cambodian ge-

ography. Cambodia is a nation of slightly less than 70,000 square miles, or approximately 181,000 square kilometers, about the size of Missouri. The majority of the country lies in the basin of the Mekong River, and it includes a heavy concentration of jungles. Phnom Penh, the capital city, lies along the Mekong in southeastern Cambodia, and Sisophon is a city in the northwest, along the border with Thailand.

- *Angkar Leu,* sometimes referred to as *Angka Loeu,* means "Higher Organization." This seems to have been the name for the higher ranks of the Khmer Rouge. Yet if someone were "sent to Angka," it seldom meant they would actually appear before high-ranking party officials; rather, this was another way of saying they would be killed.

- Long before they entered Phnom Penh on April 17, 1975, the Khmer Rouge had "liberated" other parts of

Children collect water from a bomb hole left by the Khmer Rouge on Phnom Penh, Cambodia in 1974. The Khmer Rouge forced many Cambodians living in Phnom Penh to become slaves in the rice paddies of the Cambodian countryside.
Reproduced by permission of the Corbis Corporation (Bellevue).

the Cambodian countryside and put peasants to work in slave-labor brigades. Hence the distinction between "new people" and "old people."

- In many passages from *Cambodia: Year Zero*, Ponchaud reported a sort of tit-for-tat mentality on the part of the Khmer Rouge. For instance, people were told that the Communist soldiers had "suffered ten times worse than you during the war; they had no rice and no medicine and nothing to eat but the leaves on the trees." One justification for the inhuman behavior of the Khmer Rouge toward their fellow Cambodians, then, appears to be the fact that the Khmer Rouge had suffered hardships in the process of "liberating" Cambodia.

Cambodia: Year Zero

*Almost everywhere, the work day was very long: a gong rang to wake people up around 5:00 a.m., then breakfast—rice soup—and by 6:00 everybody left for work, sometimes very far away; there was either a pause or a return to the village around 11:00, to **husk** rice and eat. Back to work from 2:00 to 5:00 p.m. or in some places 5:30 or 6:00.... [I]n other places, the refugees say that work went on at night until 8:00 or even 11:00 p.m.; when there was a moon they worked by moonlight and when there wasn't huge torches were lit.*

*All the refugees complain of the relentless, **goading** nature of the work. 'We were made to work like slaves, like beasts of burden, with no thought for the human losses!' **The human organism** was used to the extreme limit of its physical endurance; no effort was made to spare it and it was never given a day of rest.*

In some areas, work could be more immediately dangerous, because of the unexploded bombs and shells lurking in the grass or brush. In the region of Phnom Baset, northwest of Phnom Penh, a day never went by without several villagers being injured or killed by explosions.

*During the month of May people were apparently not **compelled** to work, but food was distributed in proportion to work accomplished, so the result was the same.*

Husk: Peel or shell.

Goading: Pushing, usually in a painful way.

The human organism: In other words, people's physical bodies.

Compelled: Forced or required.

Dith Pran

Dith Pran (1942–) became famous to moviegoers in the West on account of his portrayal by fellow Cambodian Haing Ngor in the movie *The Killing Fields* (1984). As a guide and interpreter working with members of the U.S. media in his country during the early 1970s, Pran got to know *New York Times* journalist Sydney Schanberg. The two became close friends, and witnessed firsthand the horrors of the Cambodian government's war with the Khmer Rouge. Pran sent his wife and four children to America, but he stayed on to help Schanberg report on the war. The Khmer Rouge took power in April 1975 and evicted all foreigners, including Schanberg.

Forced to remain in the new Cambodia, or "Kampuchea" as the Khmer Rouge had renamed it, Pran realized that he had better make himself as inconspicuous as possible. Therefore he dressed like a peasant, adopted a limited vocabulary, and pretended to be a simple villager. It was a wise decision, given the fact that the Khmer Rouge had orders to execute anyone who wore eyeglasses, perfume, makeup, watches, or other evidence of nontraditional influences. Had they learned he was an educated man who had worked closely with foreigners, Pran would have been killed instantly.

Instead he went to work, like most other Cambodians, in the rice paddies of the slave-labor camps. Their days consisted of excruciating labor, while their nights were filled with long political reeducation sessions. Though they were growing food, the ration of rice for the slaves was reduced to just one spoonful per day. Starving, Pran and other villagers ate anything they could find: bark, snakes, snails, rats, and other vermin. Some even dug up dead bodies—one of the few things that Kampuchea produced in abundance—and gnawed human flesh.

Meanwhile Schanberg had returned to the United States, where he looked after Pran's wife and children in New York City. The *New York Times* also helped support the family financially. Through intermediaries at border camps in Thailand, where Cambodian refugees fled their homeland, Schanberg circulated photographs of his lost friend with the hope that Pran had been able to flee Cambodia. In 1976, his reporting on the Cambodia earned him a Pulitzer Prize, which he accepted on behalf of Pran as well. He never stopped searching for his friend.

After the Vietnamese invasion of Cambodia in January 1979, Pran made his way to his hometown, where he found that almost all his relatives had been killed. He ultimately escaped to the Thai border, where in October 1979 he was reunited with Schanberg. Schanberg assisted Pran in relocating to the United States, where he joined his family. The *New York Times* gave him a job as a reporter, and Pran became a U.S. citizen in 1986.

At Bak Prea, on the other hand, workers who did not meet their day's quota were reprimanded, and if they did not improve they were sent to the Angkar Leu (Higher Organization) from which none ever returns.

Around Thmar Puok, during the harvest season at the end of 1975, the quota for harvesters was twenty 'heaps' a day. 'If we didn't make it,' one of them relates, 'we got only half a bowl of rice that day and had to make up the short heaps the next day. Failing to make the quota meant being sent up to the Angkar Leu.'

Between September and December the authorities began relocating large numbers of people, either to meet the requirements of the central work program or for some other, unknown reason. Hundreds of thousands of the original inhabitants of Phnom Penh.... were moved again to the Pursat, Sisophon, or Oddar Mean Chey regions. This time they were transported by truck or boat to Pursat, then to Sisophon by train.

A single account is enough to show what this second migration was like. Im Sok reached Thailand early in July 1976; he had left Phnom Penh on April 17, 1975, with his father, mother, wife, and a three-year-old daughter....

"In September 1975 the Khmer Rouge told the 'new people' and the 'old people' in some areas to assemble ... in preparation for their return to Phnom Penh. 'You don't need to take anything with you,' they told us, 'because everything has been made ready to welcome you in Phnom Penh: you will all have identical houses, equipped with everything you need.' More than thirty large trucks were waiting for us; we traveled more than a hundred to a truck. As we were getting in, the soldiers took away everything we had brought with us; all we could keep was a kettle, four tins of rice, and a bit of food for two days on the road.

"During the trip we were crushed together like a load of pigs. The trucks stopped every five or six hours to let people relieve themselves. We took Highway 2 and then Highway 3 to Phnom Penh, but then we bypassed the city center ... and the trucks turned north down Highway 5. We were all surprised at this, and everybody fell silent. It was already dark and we were still going. The children were crying and the babies screaming because they were hungry. Around eight o'clock the trucks stopped ... to let us cook some rice. At midnight we drove on again, as far as Pursat. There we were given enough rice and salt for three days. There were no camps or shelters,

so we had to sleep alongside the railroad. Several thousand people had been brought there, from all over. The sun was hardly up the next morning when the Khmer Rouge soldiers ordered us to get ready to continue the journey by train; they removed anything we had managed to keep hidden until then, and after that we had nothing but a mat, a kettle, and one plate. The train came in; we were shoved into the cars like a herd of cattle, more than a hundred and fifty to a car. After a day of traveling we reached Sisophon. From there tractors hauling trailers took some of the people to Phnom Srok; others went by oxcart. Many old people and children died on that trip, certainly not less than ten percent.

"It was growing dark. Around four o'clock the carts transporting us reached the edge of the forest near the village of Pongro in Phum Srok sector. I climbed down quickly to find shelter under a tree for my wife and child because the sky was full of threatening clouds. The Khmer Rouge handed out enough rice and salt for one day. Then the sky favored us with several downpours. We were shivering with cold, having nothing to cover ourselves with, and we looked and felt like the objects of **divine malediction**.

"The next day each family was assigned to a particular plot of land. We had to clear the ground and build cabins, each ten meters away from the next and all identical. It was the group of ten families that took charge of building the houses; we built them with the trunks of trees we **felled** in the forest and covered them with straw. There was no [water] jar, no mosquito netting, no blanket. As the Khmer saying goes, we had the ladle by the handle and the kettle by the spout, but there was nothing inside. The chief would tell us, '**The revolutionaries** suffered ten times worse than you during the war; they had no rice and no medicine and nothing to eat but the leaves on the trees.'"

According to many of the refugees this second deportation was even more deadly than the first, for people's systems were weaker and could not take the journey. A doctor, redeported from Phnom Baset to Sisophon, says that the Khmer Rouge stood, with stretchers, waiting for every train that came in to remove the dead and sick. People were **gaunt** as skeletons, their legs full of **abscesses** Another witness says that some people fell under the train on purpose to commit suicide. He speaks of 250 such suicides near Mongkol Borei. Yet another says, "On the road to Phnom Srok there were tens of thousands of people from Phnom Penh, all gaunt and lifeless, marching in columns several kilometers long. They were going to the **rice paddies** for the harvest. Some were laughing and dancing, shouting and eat-

Divine malediction: The anger or ill will of God or gods.

Felled: Cut down.

The revolutionaries: In other words, the soldiers of the Khmer Rouge.

Gaunt: Thin and bony.

Abscesses: Sores characterized by pus and inflamed tissue.

Rice paddies: Specially flooded fields where rice is grown.

Pol Pot one of the most feared leaders of the Khmer Rouge.
Reproduced by permission of AP/Wide World Photos, Inc.

Privation: A lack of the basic necessities of life.

Compulsory: Involuntary.

*ing raw rice—many had gone crazy from fatigue, **privation**, and fear."*

*Apart from the fiercely **compulsory** aspect of the work, what the deportees felt most keenly was the lack of food and inhuman discipline.*

What happened next...

Between April 17, 1975, and January 1979, when Vietnamese troops invaded Cambodia, the Khmer Rouge killed about one-third of Cambodia's estimated eight million people. This makes them the worst mass murderers in history, with a record exceeding that of Hitler's Germany, Stalin's Russia, or Mao's China.

It is easy to understand *how* the Cambodian murders occurred, given the fact that the Khmer Rouge shut their nation off from world attention. As to *why* it happened, this is a more perplexing question. To an extent, it appears that the Khmer Rouge were attempting to re-create the triumphs of the Khmer Empire, a Cambodian civilization of the medieval era that had built the vast temple complex of Angkor Wat. They believed—wrongly, according to archaeological studies of Khmer Empire lands—that the Khmer kings had built Angkor Wat and the neighboring city of Angkor Thom as giant "rice factories." To replicate these "rice factories," and to do so using the methods that would have been available to the Khmer kings in the twelfth century, the Khmer Rouge had to use slave labor.

Though many outsiders criticized the Vietnamese invasion, Cambodia was far better off under the rule of Vietnam than it had been under the Khmer Rouge. The Khmer Rouge never returned to power, though they did take part in a government formed after the Vietnamese withdrawal in 1989. By the late 1990s, the Khmer Rouge had dwindled to insignificance. In 1998, one of their most feared leaders, Pol Pot, died after being denounced by his former comrades. Few people mourned his passing.

Did you know...

- After the Thais invaded the Khmer Empire in the mid-1400s, the great temple of Angkor Wat was abandoned and eventually hidden by the jungle. It was not rediscovered until the 1860s.

- The term "killing fields" refers to the mass graves that dotted the Cambodian countryside.

- Even in the late 1990s, the per capita or average income in Cambodia was about $700 a year—less than one-fortieth of the per capita income in the United States.

For more information

Books

Ponchaud, François. *Cambodia: Year Zero*. Translated by Nancy Amphoux. New York: Holt, Rinehart and Winston, 1978.

Sources

Books

Alcraft, Rob. *Cambodia*. Des Plaines, Ill.: Heinemann Library, 1999.

Brittan, Dolly. *The People of Cambodia*. New York: PowerKids Press, 1997.

Greenberg, Keith Elliot. *Photojournalist: In the Midst of Disaster*. Photographs by John Isaac. Woodbridge, Conn.: Blackbirch Press, 1996.

Other

Beauty and Darkness: Cambodia in Modern History. http://users.aol.com/cambodia/index.htm (Accessed on May 12, 2000).

The Killing Fields (motion picture). Warner Home Video, 1984.

Huw Watkin

"Rise in Women Forced to Work as Sex Slaves"
Published in *South China Morning Post,* **August 11, 1999**

Vijay Prashad

Excerpt from "Calloused Consciences:
The Limited Challenge to Child Labor"
Published in *Dollars & Sense,* **September 1999**

All Africa News Agency

"Humanitarian Group Buys Freedom for 4,300 Sudanese"
Published in *Africa News Service,* **December 3, 1999**

In 1989 the end of communism seemed to be coming to an end; in fact, within two years the Marxist-Leninist system had been abandoned in all but a handful of countries. The exposure of crimes under particularly severe regimes, such as the one in Romania, increased international awareness of the inhumanity that persisted under communist rule.

Despite the fact that much twentieth-century slavery had been associated with communism and other totalitarian ideologies, however, the end of communism did not bring an end to slavery. (Totalitarian systems demand that people submit completely to the state, or the government.) In fact, many human rights organizations suggested that at the end of the twentieth century, more people were enslaved around the world than at any time in history.

In the last half of the twentieth century, China's economy was in the midst of a transition from an old, stagnant communist system to a hard-driving powerhouse that produced goods for export all over the world. During the 1990s, Americans became increasingly concerned that the manufactured items they bought from China and other Asian

On the edge of the 21st Century, it is unacceptable that human beings around the world are bought and sold into situations such as sexual exploitation, domestic servitude and debt bondage that are little different from slavery.... |

From "Humanitarian Group Buys Freedom for 4,300 Sudanese"

countries had been made by slave labor. The slaves included not only political prisoners in camps, but children in "sweat shops," factories in which workers labored under substandard conditions.

The articles that follow are not as famous or classic as Aristotle's *Politics* or Abraham Lincoln's Emancipation Proclamation. They are not significant legal documents, as was the case with the Code of Hammurabi or the Civil War amendments to the U.S. Constitution. They are simply three pieces out of thousands concerning slavery worldwide at the end of the twentieth century. Each article appeared in the final months of 1999, each in a different part of the world, each concerning a different variety of slavery.

The first, by journalist Huw Watkin, comes from the *South China Morning Post* in Hong Kong, and concerns the growth of sex slavery—in particular, prostitution (the practice of engaging in sex acts for hire) and the selling of "mail-order brides" (financially disadvantaged women whose prospective husbands pay to marry them)—in Southeast Asia. Second is an editorial by Vijay Prashad, a professor from India, that appeared in the U.S. economic journal *Dollars & Sense*. Speaking out against what he perceived as the dishonesty and hypocrisy of Western governments, Prashad cited the extensive use of child labor in countries of South Asia such as India and Pakistan, nations with which the United States and other Western governments had economic and political ties. Finally, the All Africa News Agency reported on perhaps the most astonishing phenomenon of all: the persistence of old-fashioned chattel slavery, in which people were literally bought and sold into lifetimes of service, just as Africans five centuries before had been.

Things to remember while reading

- The three excerpts that follow are from three different parts of the world, and represent three different perspectives. The article on sex slavery in Southeast Asia by Huw Watkin, a journalist for the *South China Morning Post* in Hong Kong, is a straight news report. This means that just the facts are reported objectively, or without inserting the writer's opinion. So is the piece from the All

Africa News Agency, a news- and information-gathering bureau with offices in Nairobi, Kenya, on the persistence of chattel slavery in Sudan. Both Hong Kong and Kenya are former British colonies; hence the use of British spellings, such as "organisation" and "programme."

- The piece by Vijay Prashad is an editorial, or opinion column, although he does use facts to support the thesis, or point, of his article. Prashad, an Indian scholar who served as assistant professor of international studies at Trinity College in Hartford, Connecticut, was not simply reporting the news, but making specific points about it. *Dollars & Sense* is a magazine on economic issues from a leftist—that is, politically nontraditional and sometimes socialist—viewpoint.

- Both the Watkin and Prashad pieces make the point that economic factors have led to the persistence of slavery. Hence Watkin reported that a United Nations official

A small group of young Asian prostitutes. In the late twentieth century sex slavery, particularly prostitution, was on the rise in Southeast Asia.
Reproduced by permission of the Corbis Corporation (Bellevue).

had "said growing prosperity in some parts of Asia was fueling the demand for commercial sex." With even greater force, Prashad made the same point, noting that—to paraphrase his quote from Karl Marx—people were getting rich off the toil of children. Marx, a German philosopher whose ideas formed the basis for communism, believed that there was an economic explanation for every event in human life.

- Traditional chattel slavery, exactly the same form of bondage in which Africans had once been captured and sold for service on plantations in the New World, continued to exist in Africa during the late twentieth century. Reports of slave trading had surfaced in many parts of northern Africa, from Mauritania in the west to Sudan in the east. The All Africa News Agency report concerns the slave-trading activity in Sudan, an outgrowth of a lengthy war between the Arab-controlled Muslim government in the capital at Khartoum and the black population of southern Sudan, who were chiefly Christian or adherents of traditional African religions. Therefore slavery in Sudan had both a racial and religious character.

"Rise in Women Forced to Work as Sex Slaves"

Young women and girls are increasingly being forced into sexual slavery abroad, with Cambodia, China and Taiwan emerging as the main markets in what welfare groups say is an increasingly serious regional problem.

*Evidence suggesting Vietnam is being targeted by the international **vice** trade is largely **anecdotal** so far, but at least three global organisations want tougher penalties and more co-operation between regional governments to stem the trade.*

Concern intensified this week when figures revealed that more than 12,000 young Vietnamese women had "married" Taiwanese men between 1996 and 1998, with close to 50 per cent of them saying they had done so for economic reasons.

Vice: Sexual immorality; in particular, prostitution.

Anecdotal: Related to anecdotes, or stories, rather than verifiable facts.

Slavery Throughout History: Primary Sources

According to an official study reported ... yesterday, the marriages were arranged by **intermediaries** for up to US $12,000... and there is growing concern about the link between "**mail-order brides**" and prostitution.

"False marriages and mail-order brides are often used as camouflage to bring women to work in overseas **brothels**, and the victims of this sort of trafficking find it difficult to argue in court that they are, in fact, victims," said Vu Ngoc Binh of Unicef [the United Nations Children's Fund].

"Huge profits can be made by forcing women into prostitution, and people-smuggling is a much less risky activity for criminals than other forms of crime, because many countries **deport** victims immediately, thereby losing valuable witnesses," she said.

Experts in the field say that despite existing **conventions**, formulating workable **domestic legislation** in order to fight the trade is difficult because Vietnamese women often enter into prostitution abroad voluntarily with the expectation of making money quickly and then getting out of the industry.

"Many women from South Vietnam are known to be working by choice as prostitutes in Cambodia," said Jette Kjertum of the International Organisation for Migration (IOM).

"But in many cases brothel owners will **confiscate** their immigration papers and force them to pay **exorbitant** commissions—basically they end up as sex slaves."

Ms. Binh said growing prosperity in some parts of Asia was fuelling the demand for commercial sex, and the IOM said China in particular was emerging as a huge market for arranged marriages.

"Men outnumber women by between 15 and 20 million in China, and with the country's emerging status as an economic power, China is set to become a major destination for trafficked women and mail-order brides," said Ms. Kjertum.

China, Cambodia and Thailand have joined a UN-sponsored project designed to stem the trade in women, but Vietnam, Laos and Burma are reported to be still considering the initiative.

Intermediaries: Go-betweens or middlemen.

Mail-order brides: Typically mail-order brides are women in developing nations who are "purchased" for marriage by men in developed nations, who pay a fee to bring them to their country.

Brothels: Houses of prostitution.

Deport: Forcibly remove.

Conventions: International agreements.

Domestic legislation: Laws within a nation, as opposed to international law.

Confiscate: Seize.

Exorbitant: Extremely expensive.

Huw Watkin, Vijay Prashad and All Africa News Agency

Although the United States and other Western countries have extensive law against the use of child labor, these countries continue to export and sell products produced in Asian sweatshops by children.
Photograph by Neil Ulevich. Reproduced by permission of AP/Wide World Photos.

Debt bondage: A situation in which a person, by incurring a debt they cannot repay, becomes a virtual slave to the person who loaned him or her the money.

"Calloused Consciences: The Limited Challenge to Child Labor"

On June 16, [U.S.] President [Bill] Clinton stood before the International Labor Organization (ILO) in Geneva and declared that "we must wipe from the Earth the most vicious forms of abusive child labor. We must put a human face on the global economy, giving working people everywhere a stake in its success."

*Two days later, the ILO finalized a new convention on the "worst forms of child labor," one that the U.S. President promised to guide through Congress. The convention targets, not all 250 million child laborers (under the age of 15) worldwide, but "all forms of slavery [of children], forced or compulsory labor, **debt bondage** and **serfdom**," child prostitution, and the use of children in the drug trade.*

*Clinton's qualified statement against the "worst forms" of child labor sounds like a coded way of telling us the United States is not opposed to the practice **per se**, but only to the "worst forms" target-*

ed in this convention by the ILO. He promises not abolition, but **amelioration**.

Yet it is not at all clear that the policies of the U.S. government, taken as a whole, will deliver even that. In June, Clinton signed an executive order preventing the U.S. government from purchasing goods made by the "worst forms" of child labor—but then exempted goods from Mexico and countries that are members of the World Trade Organization.

Or take the example of Bangladesh, where 20% of the workforce—some 6.5 million laborers—are children. In 1994, the Bangladesh Garment and Manufacturers and Exporters Association (BGMEA) agreed to eliminate child labor in its factories in the face of U.S. pressure. That pressure grew after NBC's Dateline aired a segment in 1993 on modern forms of slavery, including child labor in South Asia. After thousands of young children left the factories with **no safety net to catch them**, the U.S. government pressured the Bangladesh garment association to reverse its decision. In July 1995, the association and the United States signed a memorandum in which the employers agreed to retain the child workers and to create schools for them, but to refuse to hire any more. Meanwhile, the United States and the International Monetary Fund (IMF), which controls short-term loans to governments, were forcing the Bangladeshi government to reduce expenditures on health and education.

The United States may formally oppose child labor, but by pressing for **austerity**—especially in provision for basic needs ... it just as surely **consigns** children to the workshops and the fields. And by isolating out some children to be "saved," the United States and opponents of child labor **implicitly** suggest the **abject** poverty of the children's parents is acceptable.

The Will to Regulate

The special **abhorrence** to child labor was fed, historically, by the campaign against it in **Victorian** England. During the **Industrial Revolution**, English children worked in large numbers within factories while Indian children worked in English-owned mills in Bombay. Government action was instrumental in preventing, as Karl Marx wrote, "**the coining of children's blood into capital**." Children were rescued from the factories, not primarily in response to the onrush of **liberal** sentiment, argue scholars like Douglas Galbi, but because of the technological need for skilled adult labor instead of their unskilled toil. This shift set the stage for government regulation against

Serfdom: An institution in which peasants are forced to work the land of the wealthy.

Per se: In and of itself, or as a whole.

Amelioration: To make something more tolerable.

No safety net to catch them: In other words, no individual or group to help them meet their basic economic needs.

Austerity: Severe simplicity; in the context of economics, austerity implies spending the bare minimum.

Consigns: Relegates, or hands over.

Implicitly: Clearly.

Abject: Humiliating, or extremely low.

Abhorrence: Revulsion or rejection.

Victorian: Refers to the reign of Britain's Queen Victoria, from 1837 to 1901, or more generally to that era and its manners.

Industrial Revolution: A period of rapid development, beginning in about 1750, that transformed the economies of the West from agriculture-based to manufacturing-based systems.

The coining of children's blood into capital: In other words, the sacrifice of children's work, and indeed of their childhood, in exchange for the profits made by factory-owners.

Liberal: Characterized by a concern for the poorer classes in society.

Great Depression: A period of economic hardship in the United States, Western Europe, and other countries, between the crash of the New York stock market in 1929 and the start of World War II in the late 1930s and early 1940s.

En masse: As a group.

Artisanal: Relating to artisans, or skilled workers.

Monotonous: Repetitive and boring.

Export-oriented industries: Areas of business in which income is primarily dependent on shipping goods to other countries.

Elites: Wealthy or powerful groups.

Agrarian: Agricultural.

Redeemed: To recover ownership by paying a specified sum.

Cum: Latin for "along with being."

Traditionalist: In this context, subscribing to traditional African religions as opposed to Christianity or Islam.

Repression: Control or restraint.

Regime: Government; usually refers to a harsh or unlawful ruling group.

child labor. In the United States, it was encoded in federal law only during the **Great Depression** making an exception for agricultural labor that continues to this day.

Few places now allow children (**en masse**) to work in industrial factories. But child labor is epidemic in agriculture and in **artisanal** production. The **monotonous** tasks of the field and the small work-shop still can, and do, call upon young hands, since there are few technical skills required for the harvesting of fruit or the knotting of carpets. In India, where 11 million children work, the use of young girls in agricultural production is on the increase, according to the All-India Democratic Women's Association, as is the global use of children in the apparel industry. According to a recent U.S. Department of Labor report, children make fireworks in Peru, Mexico, and the Philippines. In Mexico, children work in garment and footwear factories. In Nepal, India, and Pakistan, children hand-knot carpets.

In India and other South Asian countries, tens of millions of children are working mostly in **export-oriented industries** (carpets, diamonds, glassware, footwear) and tourist services (including sex work) owned by local **elites**. Their labor, then, supports sectors tied to the global economy and is not a remnant of some older, **agrarian** order. It is a modern business practice, especially within nations committed to fulfilling IMF terms to cutback government programs....

"Humanitarian Group Buys Freedom for 4,300 Sudanese"

Christian Solidarity International (CSI) has bought the freedom of more than 4,300 enslaved southern Sudanese people, according to a statement released by the organisation.

"CSI **redeemed** 4,300 slaves at four locations ... paying the retrievers a fee of 50,000 Sudanese pounds equivalent to US $50," the statement said.

The statement says CSI officials John Eibner and Gunnar Wiebalck and a prominent Colorado antislavery campaigner **cum** school-teacher Barb Vogel bought the slaves between October 1-8 during a visit to the borderlands between northern and southern Sudan.

The slaves, mainly Christian and **traditionalist** women from the Dinka tribe were bought out of captivity in the Northern Sudan and returned to their homelands in the south by eight networks of Arab retrievers. To date, CSI has bought back over 15,400 slaves since the exercise started in 1995.

The statement says that all the returning slaves were captured during the raids conducted by the armed forces of Sudan's radical National Islamic Front NIF regime, in particular, its Popular Defence Force (PDF).

Slavery has been one of the **repression** tactics applied by the NIF **regime** in its quest of unleashing the **jihad** on southern Sudanese population. The civil war in the country which started in 1983 is estimated to have claimed 1.9 million people while 4 million people, mostly the Southerners, have been **displaced**.

Redeemed slaves provided the testimony to CSI personnel and accompanying independent journalists of the many gross human rights abuses that are inherent in the Sudanese slavery, the statement said.

A group of slaves gather under a tree as they wait for freedom in the southern Sudan village of Yargot after the human rights group Christian Solidarity International paid for their freedom.

Reproduced by permission of Reuters/Stringer/Archive Photos.

Jihad: Arabic for "holy war"; refers to the Muslim belief that war on behalf of Islam, or against believers in other religions, is a godly act.

Displaced: Forced to leave one's home.

The Arab Slave Trade

The majority of slaves brought to the New World between the mid-1400s and the mid-1800s came from West Africa. Yet just as slavery was abolished in the Americas, a new trade in slaves from East Africa was just beginning. This time the slave traders were primarily Arabs, and the markets in which they sold their slaves were in the Middle East, India, and even China.

Long before Europeans began buying and selling slaves, Arab slavers had conducted a profitable slave trade. This trade entered a second phase around the same time the United States and other countries outlawed slavery. America had certain ideals about freedom, human dignity, and the rights of individuals, ideals that made the persistence of slavery in the southern United States a glaring dichotomy. By contrast, most nations in the Arab world did not place the same kind of value on individual human lives—particularly the lives of foreigners and people who did not embrace the Islamic religion. Thus the slave trade in the Middle East did not raise the same kinds of emotional issues as slavery in America had.

Making a base at Zanzibar, an island off the east coast of Africa that is now part of Tanzania, Arab slavers in the mid-1800s began moving into the interior, capturing slaves for sale in the Zanzibar markets. An estimated 20,000 to 40,000 slaves a year passed through Zanzibar, some bound for service in Arabia and other far-off lands, some put to work on the island's plantations.

Among the most prominent East African slave traders was Tippu Tib (about 1837–1905), a merchant of mixed Arab and black African heritage. Ironically, Tippu Tib's move inland, which led to the enslavement of many people, provided the justification for Leopold's takeover of the Belgian Congo. Leopold's reign proved to be far worse for the locals than Tippu Tib's slaving raids had been.

Another important Arab slave-trading center was in Egypt, as slavers went southward from Egypt into the Sudan. Missionaries, or religious teachers, from Europe helped put an end to this trade, yet by the end of the twentieth century, Arabs from northern Sudan were once again buying and selling black Africans from southern Sudan. This activity was part of a larger war between the country's Arab Muslim government and its black majority, who were either Christians or adherents of traditional African religions.

War booty: Treasures taken by victors in battle.

*It added: "During the raids, villages are torched, men are shot dead, the elderly are beaten and abused and women, children, cows, goats and food stores are captured as **war booty**. The women and children are forced to walk for days to the North."*

On the way, beatings, public executions and gang rape are commonplace, witnesses say. In the North, the slaves are divided among their captors. They are routinely subjected to forced labour, sexual abuse, forced **Islamisation**, beatings, death threats and meagre diet.

The Khartoum government and the United Nations Children's Fund (UNICEF) Executive Director Carol Bellamy are spearheading the campaign against the redemption of Sudanese slaves. They have condemned CSI and the victimised Dinka community for violating the 1926 Slavery Convention, which prohibits **trafficking** in human beings.

However, Dinka Chiefs and a section of observers continue to support the role played by CSI in freeing the slaves. They accuse UNICEF of condemning the CSI while doing little to stop the menace despite the UN agency's vast resources.

CSI's International President Reverend Hans Stuckelberger confirmed during a BBC [British Broadcasting Corporation] World Service broadcast last month that CSI intends to continue its slave redemption programme and broader anti-slavery campaign until the last Sudanese slave has been freed.

Hans also appealed to United Nations General Secretary Kofi Annan to take all the necessary and urgent steps to immediately stop slavery and other related "crimes against humanity" that are being committed by the government of Sudan and its agents.

Last month, 14 women Foreign Ministers, among them United States Secretary of State Madeleine Albright, petitioned Annan seeking an end to the widespread trafficking in women and children.

"On the edge of the 21st Century, it is unacceptable that human beings around the world are bought and sold into situations such as sexual exploitation, domestic servitude and debt bondage that are little different from slavery," the Ministers noted.

Other petitioners were from South Africa, Niger, Madagascar, Bahamas, Barbados, Bulgaria, Salvador, Finland, Liechtenstein, Luxembourg and Sweden.

Islamisation (or Islamization): Conversion to Islam.

Trafficking: Trading or selling.

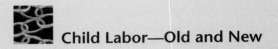

Child Labor—Old and New

The Industrial Revolution, a period of rapid development that transformed agriculture economies to manufacturing economies, began in England around 1750. This was a painful transition, as economic needs forced many people to leave farms and the countryside to move to the city. There they toiled for long hours in dirty, smelly factories; and at night these workers went home to sleep in extremely substandard quarters.

Among the hardest-hit victims of industrialization were children. Poverty forced many working-class children into the grim, gloomy sweatshops of nineteenth-century England. These years produced many horrible scenes of six-year-olds forced to labor like adults; of children who lost fingers or hands in dangerous machinery; of youngsters who worked twelve or sixteen hours a day, six days a week.

As the nineteenth century progressed, industrialization—and the evils associated with it—spread to Germany, France, and other nations of the European continent, as well as to the United States. In many of these countries, children had worked on a family farm, or at least on a plot of ground that the family tilled together. In contrast, the factories separated children from parents, wives from husbands, and so on.

Given the negative side effects, it is easy to conclude that industrialization did not improve the lives of working-class people. Yet that conclusion is based on the

What happened next...

Watkin and Prashad made a valuable point in their observation that economics drives slavery. Without men pouring money into the sex-slave industry, and without Westerners purchasing goods produced by slave labor in developing lands, slavery would not exist.

Over time, the ideas surrounding slavery have differed, ranging from the typically nonracist practices of ancient times to the highly racist institutions of the early modern era; or from the political slavery of Nazi Germany to the sexual slavery of child-pornography rings in the late twentieth century. Yet economic needs have almost always been a driving force.

A particularly troublesome example of slavery and economics involves efforts by CSI to purchase people out of bondage in Sudan. On the one hand, these efforts are unques-

short-term impact of industrialization, not the long-term effects. It is because of industrialization and the forces that motivated it, for instance, that scientists are able to develop life-saving medicines, which pharmaceutical companies then produce and sell to the public. Furthermore, the transition from agriculture to industry in the United States helped ensure that a slave-based economy such as that of the South would never be an issue again.

The Industrial Revolution was a huge societal change, but it did not last. Eventually England absorbed the effects of the transition, and rising humanitarian concerns forced a number of changes—including child-labor laws. The United States adopted its own series of laws prohibiting child labor in the years between 1900 and 1930.

During the late twentieth century, industrialization spread to underdeveloped countries such as India. Unfortunately, with it came even greater abuses of child labor. This situation prompted Vijay Prashad's critique of child-labor practices in *Dollars & Sense*. In Prashad's opinion (and that of scholar Douglas Galbi, referred to by Prashad), Western nations did not end child labor for humanitarian reasons, but simply because of changes in the economy. There is no doubt a great deal of truth in this. In fact, it is probably a combination of both economic changes and humanitarian concerns that prompts reforms such as child-labor laws.

tionably admirable, representing the best in the Western and Christian tradition of respect for human life. On the other, as many critics have charged, CSI's offer of payment to slave traders only gives them greater incentive to capture and sell more humans. It is also disturbing that the UN seems to have sided with the government of Sudan in condemning CSI for violating laws against buying slaves—when in fact it is the Sudanese government that makes it possible for people to purchase slaves.

For slavery to end in Sudan, or India, or China laws will have to change. Yet before laws can change, or at least before they can become effective, change will have to occur in people's hearts. If the world ever becomes a place in which everyone respects the rights of others, slavery will wither away and die for good.

Did you know...

- In 1996, controversial Nation of Islam leader Louis Farrakhan (1933–) visited a number of countries, including Sudan, on a world tour. Many observers criticized him for visiting a country in which black people were enslaved, and Farrakhan publicly denied that slavery existed in Sudan. To prove that this was not true, two reporters for the *Baltimore Sun* traveled to Sudan in August 1996, purchased two slaves, and freed them.

- In the 1990s, slavery reappeared in what had been one of the largest slave societies of the 1800s: Brazil. There many thousands of unfortunate people became victims of kidnaping and other scams to place them in varieties of bondage ranging from debt slavery to sex slavery. Among these were Indians enslaved in charcoal mines, where children as young as nine worked for twelve hours a day in extremely hazardous conditions.

- The U.S. Department of Health and Human Services (HHS) reported in the 1990s that there were as many as 300,000 child prostitutes—some as young as nine years of age—in the United States.

For more information

Periodicals

All Africa News Agency. "Humanitarian Group Buys Freedom for 4,300 Sudanese." Africa News Service, December 3, 1999.

Prashad, Vijay. "Calloused Consciences: The Limited Challenge to Child Labor." *Dollars & Sense,* September 1999, p. 21.

Watkin, Huw. "Rise in Women Forced to Work as Sex Slaves." *South China Morning Post,* August 11, 1999.

Sources

Other

The American Anti-Slavery Group. http://www.anti-slavery.org (Accessed on May 12, 2000).

Amnesty International. http://www.amnesty.org (Accessed on May 12, 2000).

Anti-Slavery International. http://www.antislavery.org (Accessed on May 12, 2000).

Christian Solidarity International. http://www.csi-int.ch/ (Accessed on May 12, 2000).

Human Rights Watch. http://www.hrw.org (Accessed on May12, 2000).

International Labor Organization. http://www.ilo.org (Accessed on May 12, 2000).

United Nations High Commissioner for Human Rights. http://www.unhchr.ch/html/intlinst.htm (Accessed on May 12, 2000).

Index

Bold type indicates main
entries and their page
numbers. Illustrations are
marked by (ill.).